As She Returns Now

STEINBERG HENRY

First Edition: 2009
Front Cover Design: Book Vine Press
Back Cover Concept: Steinberg Henry
Back Cover Photograph: Henrick Aaron
Author's Photograph: Greg John-Baptiste

ISBN 978-1-954941-34-2 (softcover)
ISBN 978-1-954941-35-9 (ebook)

Printed in the United States of America.

Book Vine Press
2516 Highland Dr.
Palatine, IL 60067

Daisy Augusta Andrew, March 31, 1922–August 5, 2003

Mother's Name: Civilia Andrew nee Vidal

Grandfather's Name: David Vidal

Father's Name: Edward Andrew

Grandfather's name: Prince Andrew

SPONSORS (godparents): Albert Casey & Maudry Riviere

DEDICATION

To my brothers Albert and Ernest and their children.

To my sisters Pearl and Joycelyn and their children.

To the memory of Teddy, our brother Bernard, and our sisters Eudora, Ketturah and their children.

To Tony and his children

To Desmond, Casandra, Tessa and Jeffrey and their children.

To my children Zev, Glendora, Imran and Roberta and their children.

To Jeanne who was a true daughter-in-law to our Mother.

To Caesarina Paul for her magnificent rendition of the Twenty-Seventh Psalm -- my Mother's favourite.

ACKNOWLEDGMENT

Many, many thanks to my wife and children for supporting me as I wrote this interpretation of mourning.

Thanks to my brothers and sisters for just being there.

Thanks to Berge and Family for giving me shelter in New York's 2003 Autumn and Winter.

Ross Loramol provided an excellent interpretation of those Dominican expressions appearing in this text. Anyone working in the world of Translation and Interpretation can count on Ross' professionalism. He is exceptional in the use of the French language.

Greg John Baptiste clicked my photograph even as he raised philosophical issues for a fascinating afternoon discourse.

I will be forever thankful to the community in which I grew up and was cultured: Zicack, Portsmouth, Dominica, East Caribbean.

…and when we embark on the path of death, renewal, and rebirth.
It is her song, singing in our blood and our soul, that inspires us
—Isis.

I will lead the blind by ways they have not known, along
unfamiliar paths I will guide them; I will turn the darkness
into light before them and make the rough places smooth
—Isaiah 42:16 (NIV).

There is no struggle of soul and body save in the minds of those
whose souls are asleep and whose bodies are out of tune
—Kahlil Gibran, Sand And Foam.

NOTE ON THIS EDITION

In 2009, a book was in my hand and it was mine! But the work was fraught with errors and those who cared to print, design and cover its pages did not concern themselves with the text, its syntax, its spellings, its standardization. I too made errors. For example remind was typed "rmind;" Isaiah was typed as "Isiah" and steep was closer on the keyboard. It was typed "dteep." I should've checked those, but I was new to the screen-reader Jaws. I did not always catch its nuances if we can refer to its machine-driven pronunciation as presenting nuances. Honestly, I thought those printing and covering the book would at the very least check the typos they were putting out. But, as they said, it was my responsibility to at least spell-check.

The text, as it was, was overwhelming even to me its writer since I was not reading with my eyes, but was listening to it. It was a new, yet refreshing learning development tool for me; one that I became better at by the time of my second publication in 2011.

I believe that a word should be written correctly. Yes, I hope you find this edition clean and representative of the woman, the culture it is designed to present.

Then there was the issue of punctuation. The style emerging in this book was my deliberate choice. It is one I am still trying to perfect if ever. I say if ever because I am constantly experimenting with and learning from long flowing sentences in which words connect using few conjunctions causing the reader to read on fearlessly if you wish coming upon two words which in usual sentence structuring would require a comma or punctuation but in this case the reader is the one interrogated somewhat, yes, asked to place in the mark or read the text as if she/he knows a comma should be there. Here are a few examples.

In Chapter Twelve you find "{B}etween Dominica and New York Mama between your resting place and where I am, is an ocean itself rattling bones reparation rhythms your daughters remains in salt and algae, shelves rocks; sunken master helmsmen's notes, broken wheels, sharks dolphins whales, healing elements, coral calcium, the slime in conch, Haitian bones, sponges, half of sails, rudders skills, decks shafts wheelhouses treasures, what we called bullion at high-school, Kalinago pots, rigs, compasses. There is fire too in salt. You grieved as she crossed frontiers of oceans caught in currents between the Caribbean Sea and the Atlantic."

There are what I call "runs" in this sentence where two or three words could've been separated by a comma, but I choose not to. Along the way you read of "'an ocean itself rattling bones reparation rhythms your daughters remains in salt and algae." Bones, reparation, and rhythms could be separated by commas but I allow the sentence to run. Also, in that sentence you read "broken wheels, sharks dolphins whales, healing elements, coral calcium" and more. Observe the "sharks dolphins whales" without a comma between them. This is the exercise in rhythm in flow that I keep perfecting. The reader notices the absence but reads on to find the words read as if the punctuation is present. In some instances, readers have stopped, finding the flow odd, uncovering what seems to be a fault in constructing the sentence. You were called on to participate in construction of that sentence. It is a strange requirement given that the modern reader does not want to do much interpretation in these times. I suggest that not only do you read the text; you participate in how it sounds. Yes, sounds! The critic in you reading opens its judgement, suspends its judgement so to speak to allow the writer some freedom; to discover the writer's person communicating, suggesting an additional way of reading. Here's another sentence from Chapter Twenty-Four.

"{T}his narrative is at one point technical at another ecopoetic on death expanding the reduced to The general living, daring on account of the fact that I'm writing about my Mother to telescope Networks such as families races nations largely on my understanding of issues shared during conversations with her." Observe "families races nations."

Here's one colorful frame drawn from Chapter Thirty-Three when I reached the public market in Dominica's capital, Roseau. Notice its run. "{B}asille peppermint rosemary parsley jelly-nuts carrots, green yellow red white purple flowers, breadfruits breadnuts dasheen were in abundance though much less than what it used to be ten years ago." That was 2003! This is Waitukubuli and invariably, just as this island shatters perception and amazes with its historic fecundity, there are additional surprises. I say, welcome to this other reading!

CONTENTS

DOMINICAN EXPRESSIONS

Bear in mind that Dominican Words as you highlight them are the resulting fusion of French, English and Indigenous cross references and communication conveniences, as individuals over the years have sought to convey their messages by whatever construct or deformation facilitated said exchanges. This conveying of messages, this exchange of meanings, mattered more than paying attention to grammar and any kind of correct spelling...since for the most part and even still today, the Dominican way of communication is exclusively an oral form.

1. The Oral expression "Kwedi" with a French acute accent on "e", means an understanding between relatives and friends and neighbors that allows one the privilege of benefitting from goods and services that could be paid for by barter or cash at a later moment in time
2. Déjà—a standard French word which means already
3. Plus—The Dominican word is actually spelt "pli" and "plis" but is understood to mean more. The word is actually a deformation of the term "plus" in French, as the locals tried to listen and memorize and repeat what they thought they heard from their masters
4. Lagli—local colloquial term meaning any sticky sap from the bark of trees or from leaves
5. Julie—or grafted mango is the name given to a local juicy mango grown throughout the island

6. Kakapool—is actually two words conveniently juxtaposed for conveying a specific message. One word is kaka which means excrement and the other word is pool which means free range chicken or fowl. The word kaka can then be linked to the generator of excrement. Example the word moun (pronounced moon) means people or human beings and so kakamoun would mean human excrement
7. Long is the name for locally found slender-looking sweet mango
8. Leeckah is the name of yet another variety of local sweet mango which has characteristic, small black spots when fully ripe
9. Teetoo is the name of yet another variety of local mango which has a characteristic sharp tingy taste on the tongue
10. Mouleng is the name of yet another variety of local juicy mango with a very thin skin and which gives a fleshy mouthful
11. Kouliw a very popular seasonal fish
12. Koud'main derived from the French "coup de main"—Coup has been deformed and now has a 'k' instead of a 'C'. The original French word "coup" means blow and "main" means hand. Coup de pied means a blow with the foot =kick, coup de tete means blow with the head = head butt or smart brain strategy. Koud'main means literally blow with the hand but this time the blow is inflicted on manual tasks at hand, whereby many hands join in and assist in bringing a project to completion at no charge to the benefactor except that of providing food and drink
13. Fatpoke—a pod containing seeds covered by a white, sweet flesh that children sucked
14. Kashima—a sugar-apple

15. Diable—you may use the standard French term it means the same and spells the same and from which comes Diablesse, which the locals feel was the female to the male diable
16. Soucouyant is our version of what the Americans call witch on a broom flying at night, except that theirs may be fictitious, but ours are real women as part of our lives superstition
17. The Kalinago race or Carib people as they were formerly called, are the 3500 remnants of the 'indigenous' people living on the North Eastern side of the island of Dominica in their Kalinago Territory
18. Bouyon. Dominican music genre combining traditional and modern music technology and sensibilities into one dynamic rhythm.

Ross Loramol, Commonwealth of Dominica
Bilingual & Interpretation Services -- ____________

CHAPTER 1

Pulse out of New York

As I reflect on her beauty, fond laughter burps in me, a cool gathering-up suggesting purification time, a will to restoration of simple ways, a back to basics representation. She was going on to being one again with the Earth. I was to remain here. I am to lift her spirit in me to the highest high.

Though blinded by glaucoma, she was not a sickly woman. However during the final year of her eighty-one years on Earth, she had her womb removed because of an issue of blood, the doctor fearing traces of cancer. Then she fell and fractured her hip. None of us her children were told the extent of blood vessel damage in her pelvis among other complications. Although her mobility was limited by visual impairment, at that time in our part of the world, that fracture meant permanent immobility. By then, she must have felt the end coming, but never discussed that transition, preferring rather to remain in silence, choosing instead every minute of Life. That was her life -- a life that chose Life. What mattered in this sojourn of eighty-one years, was work, earning a living helping others, treating hunger with immediacy. She was not airy-fairy. When she finally turned to herself, she had already nurtured, cultured patterns of overcoming. She felt the pain, but looked beyond. She had felt another kind of pain all her life, one mingled with pleasure, joy, profound sense of achievement, frustration, loss, but always moved to overcoming through acts of kindness. I stood at her grave-side and could not be sad.

Now seated in a house in Queens, New York, I reflect on her passing, the funeral service and, throughout this recollection, her words. It is from this place in time that I reflect on our times, conversations, how she nurtured us. It is from New York that I journey through her ideas and mine touching glaucoma, motherhood, living in a Dominican ecology as a boy; indeed living in a Caribbean culture, overcoming, the struggle between Life and Death, dying, her religious belief, her spiritual life, her active call for silence.

CHAPTER 2

After News of Mama's Death

I left Dominica in November 2002, and though I tried to speak with my Mother by telephone from New York, I still believe that my leaving Dominica grieved her. This is one of the weights in the scales of mourning. We had spoken so abundantly throughout her life, that when I visited her in May 2003 and for seven days she would not speak with me I recognized a figure in transformation. I observed two faces melting into one. One side was drawn and skeletal, the other dark. Then the two would become one with brilliance and a look of having won. A drifting was taking place. I would return to New York, disturbed. Three months later she died. We had not shared any meaningful words since November 2002 when I left Dominica for New York. Attempts at speaking with her by telephone proved difficult since she would either mumble, not appear to hear or do what I thought was listening only to respond with a cryptic amorphous cry, a moan, and finally a sigh of relief. I could not tell.

My mind and soul were even more affected, thrown into turmoil when I visited in May 2003, when she chose to teach me power in silence. I was turned inside out and outside in, even upside down.

For me it was total, another arrangement, another struggle site, vista, sanctuary if you would permit. I was bursting through another water-bag.

So, after news of her death, because of what I felt shifting inside, I was convinced that my Mother who carried me had to be a most interesting woman beyond her overt simplicity and lightness of being. My thoughts began fanning. I could not let go of her life. I rested back a little. There must be another place for her. Maybe I could find comfort in those thoughts. This is Mother. I can take the latitude to think through ages and ages of becoming. She served as a body for my body. My body and hers were connected by cords carrying blood. My heart beat in her. I breathed in her, rooted in her, the essence of my being blossomed in her. Indeed, mourning was not going to be just dressing in black staying away from dances, parties. There was more to be harvested in this time, this season. What if I could imagine what was happening to her as she changed in her burial spot. That seemed an exercise in futility. Perchance, I thought, there is a philosophical entry to this idea of returning to oneness to Earth and its fullness. That sounded better. Philosophy would take me part of the way, so would rationality. I didn't want to imagine only. Historical methodology had taught me that imagination coupled with fact generated fruitful results. I needed to think. I mused: an introductory knowledge of physiology or anatomy is necessary. But would these matter to, in death? What about poetry? I recall spontaneously what Caribbean poet Derek Walcott called the carrion and the world of forgotten historic mansions -- wrought iron broken wheels cold fire places mills and tools. In Walcott's poem death was everywhere at structural and super-structural levels. I search memory now for micro and macrocosmic anatomical ferences to alert me, finding trace artifact in wood iron steel rubber forest and underground. I interpreted, felt rush of spirit in those remains. There must have been sentience, blood bone. Spirit of Poetry would give me Fire. With Poetry I could leap, juxtapose unfamiliars, give form to otherwise unformed imaginaries. I took to wondering -- what if a sharing, an exchange began. Would I now be indulging in communication beyond the rational, the logical? Would my poetry be communicating with the dead? What if Mother and Son were connected to the extent that her death and return signified, sparked his rebirth, his restoration and as she melts into the Earth he follows her unfolding organs and releases his fears whether they be of decay, disease and death devils or childhood spirits? The psychological would not be a sufficiently strong dam, though necessary as a first source, maybe the place from which to begin to grapple with Mama's longing, thirst, hunger. She thirsted and hungered after righteousness. Righteousness? We don't know these Caribbean, West Indian women fighters in the Spirit whom gender differences did not inhibit. But for now, for her, all is over, all pain gone all disorders wiped away all doubts dissipated all troubles laid down.

In her living days, she would have taken those troubles, issues to the Lord in prayer. This Lord was not British, neither was he a keeper of serfs, slaves and large estates in colonies. The Lord she spoke of in her living years was The Anointed One, Jesus of the line of David hailing to Abraham, Isaac and Jacob.

People of my Mother's generation were long-distance runners; they did not have to get into the promise land on Earth. They simply had to see it or evidences of it. They prayed hard, investing, they said, in their children. They thought of leaving not only the material, but the blessing, good works, a good name. When you have children?

Mother was so steeped in song and Psalm-chanting that truly, it is impossible to leave out her morning and evening glorification. It is also difficult not to question justice's trickle, its unexpected arrival, its arrival in its own time, its seeming disappearance into the meshwork of an economic arrangement calling on all partaking in it to be obedient. Christ Jesus living in the Caribbean is a phenomenon to behold. Personally, if you wish, I have found Christ Jesus to be the most wonderful figure I've read about in the wisdom traditions. They even told me that he lives in my heart. He died and yet lives. He is like a seed that dies first to break forth. His spirit lives in a Caribbean person, though he was a Jew. Who is the Jew? He died for the sins of a Caribbean Mother, though he lived in what is now called the Middle East. Was this once Africa? Could he have visited India, South America and Mainland Africa? Could he have sojourned in China and Tibet? Could he have sailed through the Caribbean long before Columbus, seen the Kalinago and walked on water to the joy of Incas, Aztecs and Mayas? The story of Christ Jesus is wonderfully interesting. He was/is God made flesh, -- he rules over a Kingdom that is in me. Interesting, is it not? Mama, this could not be the historical Christ after the Roman idea, neither could it be the theological one after Europe's adventure. Christ has to be boundless, giving us all the power in the spirit to do like him, as he said, greater than him -- find in us that resurrection power, that healing strength. I believe people of my Mother's generation had glimpses of this spirit of discovery and liberation, that spirit of being in the universe not simply subject to things, events and times. Self-exploration in light of Mama's death? What could be better. I was going to need a child's imagination, one that did not know fear, yet respected his parents. I needed hummingbird speed-- I could not hesitate. Somewhere someone had died. Could I safely say it was for me? I say this because I was beginning to believe that this was a serious challenge. I had not been to or in this zone prior to this passing, but her dying almost commanded me: I could do more than mourn or wait for the season of dancing. It's a new literary space. It is a non-objective matter. This would not have emerged if Mama hadn't died.

I realized the event would change my relation to Thought and writing -- I wanted to write and not be encumbered by rules telling me where I could and could not trod. At the same time I had to be responsible: it was a maturing experience. Where would it lead? How could I say that she died for me. I was not her only child. I was not the first neither was I the last. Truth is, her death called me to remembrances of us all. So though I'd rather have the text flow seemingly having a life of its own and going where it chose, I had to honor the life of this woman in whose body I was fearfully and wonderfully formed. I was born through her, drawn from her water, the unspoken in my eyes inscribed on her bosom daily. When she gave up her body the spiritual woman emerged in full. This woman's spirit and more is my friend. In her religious and spiritual tradition, the ovarian release which brought her birth knew her time of death. As she returns again, she connects to that moment when she herself was conceived -- her life having been mapped out long before conception by a master cartographer. In her spiritual practice, the season of her birth was known, so was the precise time. Her purpose for taking form here was known. When she left this stage, this scene, this act, this visibility, she had already fed her children and those of others. She had fathered her children as if there were no other interests. She had struggled through heartbreaks, disappointments in relationships, emerging proud, a fighter, a warrior, never leaving her children without, having the capacity to work, to spread love within her camp without lifting her voice, seldom lifting her hand. Tolerant to the bone, Mama considered herself a Christian, though from my experiences being with her, I am assured that she remains a spiritual actor not a religious one. What else could a woman born in a 1920s Caribbean be? Christian? To this day, and more so following her death, I am convinced that the problem of the Caribbean woman and man is not salvation of the soul but rather critical mental emancipation, essentially salvaging of an economic and material mode of production. I am convinced that in part she knew this. Somehow she knew that her struggle was within a system bred in religiosity and inequity. She also knew another front transcending flesh and blood. So while she was inspired to creative business, she wrestled with forces in that space between spirit and body to secure healing, to extract cure. Why would the Spirit have responded, responded to every other desire she had, save the one for return of her sight? Seek first the Kingdom of Heaven/God, and all else shall be added/given to you. Did the system of colonial control keep people of her generation so focused, so stuck on making a living that their thoughts and emotions were bound to Earth? Those owning material means for purchasing labor did not at the same time realize interconnectedness between acts of justice on Earth and in Heaven. In their consciousness then, the Universe was not one. Think of it -- what better place but under the Sun? Opposition to my Mother's peoples Earth-Heaven knowingness was direct, intense, anxiety-laden, oftentimes criminal. How did they fly over those seasons of inequality and injustices? What of those wet days of kwédi, those times of credit? It was sharing. It was love. Their community spirit transcended individual wants, personal needs. In each other's communion, in meaningful commensality, they found anointing.

One thing is for sure: they were fascinating interpreters of the times. Not only did they live long; they carried, presented their sufferings to their Lord Christ. They even gave thanks for the outcome whether they were made better or became worst till death. To me however, the movement between spirit and body could have drawn her out of blindness. Was this meant to be? Is there a disease that is meant to be, or should body not be transformed by thought, by spirit rising? This is no longer her generation's to answer. This is my dance, my technology, my reward from Mama's love, Mama's protection. Should the disconnect between spirit and body, prayer, meditation and its effect on body be trivialized? Not at all. It is for me an arc of interest in this mourning blitz. So many of our people never realized the connect though they cried out, though they had every strand of evidence that it existed. It is in this gap that I run drawing meaning from two sentences, maybe three, five, taut in psychological tension, raft, caught between river and sea current, for one moment standing still until releasing its magnetic field to the attraction of the larger issue of liberty, transcendence, restoration, dancing. It says something to us living, those left to witness, to experience return. It says you must live. It says stand for something. It says care yourself, know yourself, culture learning, care your off-spring. It is this knowing that we all must die, yet instructing that we care ourselves that invests life, living with value, but also with a mystique, a mystery shifting behind our sunburnt skin, behind a stone, in a cave on a mountain-side, in the context of a lionesses' prowess. Lioness? Certainly, she was not afraid to defend her cubs, neither was I afraid of her dead body.

When the family went to see her at the funeral home I gently pressed the center of her forehead. I needed to touch her. She was cold. I had seen her almost three months before. I should've been crying, weeping. I should be grieved. I wasn't. As the body was revealed, my heart skipped. Then her face. Calm, almost girlish. My God!

One of the wonderful things about having grandchildren visit the funeral home, particularly when they travelled from other countries to attend the funeral, is that they cushion the grief. Younger people, children just look on, knowing in their souls a subtle call to continuity. They just looked on as we negotiated formalities, you know, casket quality and price, whether we wanted the body gently lowered and ensuing costs. Grief is lightened by these matter-of-fact responsibilities. We have to be focused putting our loved-ones away. Those who speak with us at the funeral home, have spoken with so many people and they're into the business of burial. But the grandchildren were chuckling, enjoying the afternoon out, taking the hurt away.

As we drove back home to Portsmouth, her children and grandchildren in a huge rented bus, I began to want to know what was in her cold liver, her entrails now. The place wherein I took shape, gathered up form in the flesh, was dead, yet I was alive. Intriguing relation, is it not? Doesn't this life have to do with more than flesh and blood, death and dying? I am becoming aware that these surges are going to continue throughout this text. There was not going to be an autopsy, but even such intrusions could not find a word for me in its probe and plumb. She in that physical state I just left at the funeral home, seemed released, relieved, deprived of a sweet burden considering that these women born in the 1920s and early 1930s always sought a challenge, another creative way to sustain income, to nourish and clothe children, to themselves still look good and in many instances, cook for and entertain a man. They worked hard over and beyond the call to sustain their own persons. These women had little; they were pure actors of faith. Yet, they were deprived of cure, albeit physically. I speak here not about cure from physical injury caused by falling, but in the case of Mama, of the cry posted by Luke and Isaiah: he sent me... to tell blind people that they can see. It is this promise she anticipated, since Jesus Christ whom Isaiah proclaimed, is the same today, yesterday and tomorrow. With such timelessness qualities, I thought of the Christ-Spirit knowing everything, every spot and blip in the human body, every cell, each protein, each amino acid's fiery expression, each messenger, each silent drop of blood trickling up or down the cardio. Jesus, the Word made Flesh? Jesus rose Lazarus from the dead, from a place where he stank, from a place where doctors never go -- almost as if death were a disease requiring the medicine concocted only in the laboratory of Divine Spirit. Christ Jesus is said to know each thought, intention. Could he not have poured out a refreshing chemistry in her brain to the rebuilding, the reconstitution of the optic nerve, the retinal ganglion cells? Could his Spirit have catalyzed, spirited a thought? Thoughts are not visible. Do they not contain energy and the Christ-Body an abundance of the same? I was so moved by her passing, I began to ask why is it that Christ Jesus who knows the entire body and thought composition, does not heal it when his people, our people cry out. Imagine this. Think of the box owned by Pandora opening. I was in danger, in trouble now. Thing is, my Mother's generation of women were too busy to challenge doctors treatments, to search them out, to question them, even attempt to think about a similarity of origin that medicine might have with their traditional religious and healing practices. Furthermore, ritual had in many cases taken the place of spontaneous prayer. But girl when Mama chanted Psalms, she chanted. Even if tainted by ritual, she was consistent in her departure from ritual, chanting Psalms back to back, maybe to the point where she did not listen. But I am convinced beyond doubt that as she worked, her bones and thoughts were full of those ancient words. She just didn't have a harp, or stringed instrument accompanying her plaintivity. How the Merciful God, King of Kings, Lord of Lords, Conquering Lion of the Tribe of Judah did not hear her cry for sight, baffles me still.

Driving that afternoon through Dominica's verdant green, I found myself reflecting inevitably on rising tones of Ethiopia's Falasha musicians as they touch King David's mystical body and symbolic harp in the service of liberation to Jews of all races, even those of the East whom the world still needs to know. But this hopeful sound and thought-path is geographically distant from Dominica's trans-insular road, though not disconnected by way of humanity's common thread, sounding its tenderness at the base of the belly. This notion of Falasha virgin harmony is just outside my echo threshold. Truly, this Judaic thought-web hangs now in tandem with a gentle Caribbean afternoon, driving with family through wonderful verdant green, brown, yellow, sunlight and diverse family of trees, shadows and breeze on an island too warm for the funeral home's ice, too tropical for Robert Frost.

CHAPTER 3

Drifting Adolescent Recollections

On the day of her burial as I looked over her laying in state at the entrance to the Portsmouth Catholic Church, Dominica, I touched, appreciated her hairstyle. She had this bulky bunch of silver hair neatly wrapped and slightly parted over the right side. After having peeped at the body at the church's entrance, one of the town's characters shouted to me, "your Mother looking splendid!"

There is an awesome path to be cut here: overall She was well done. The Methodists would cant, thou good and faithful servant. She carried a calm resolve that was not an end in itself, adding to her splendor. Beyond this architecture that I saw resting in a varnished box was a phenomenon. I looked to the weather. I needed to give meaning to going over, this journeying to meet her Maker, as they would say, this passing on, this letting go.

Today was not a normal working day when she left in the morning and came back in the evening sometimes in the night or early hours of the morning, looking silently over us all before resting into sleep. But she came back. This time around, Mama as we knew her in the flesh would not be back. My Father's passing twenty-seven years earlier, had not generated such emotions, the no return affair. She who had clothed my body was now gone.

It rained that morning of the day on which she was laid to rest. I remember hoping it would not rain during the afternoon's internment and it didn't. That was beyond me. I burst into tears when the body disappeared in the flow of the cortege realizing that she was no longer our property. The woman with whom I sat in private, fed, laughed with, was now community property being moved through streets, dispatched with such speed. Within thirty minutes Mama was being covered. The structure we and community knew in person had to be reconstituted, the resting place remodeled refurbished. Comfort had to be sought otherwise. Here there was no longer a light-house no chain no raft. All would be reformulated and beautifully too, especially when the tools were, and are fashioned after ancestral values, the Ancient of Days.

Truly, it was not possible to wail over the return of an eighty-one year old woman. This life had been well lived and was, according to my sister Joycelyn, on its way to Heaven. The priest who developed the homily knew, understood that to get there, she had to die in Christ. I did not want a futile religious debate. The woman I knew as Mama preferred in place of a debate, hard work, prayer, faith hope charity.

From the dawn of my early mourning, I could hear her: the less you talk the more you see. Stay out of religion and politics. If politics is concerned Mama, with power, influence and authority and religion points to an entry, a point of connection to spiritual growth and development, then I understand the responsibility to reach and keep the higher end of that ethical ground. In fact, and that is on reflection, her suggestion that I stay away from political and religious debates, prepared me for a deeper, broader grasp of the political. She was being political when she sought to influence my lifestyle. Mothers are not party political as much as they are naturally political. She tolerated political discourse that did not lash out, one that presented a solid human critique. She did not trust the look in my unruly knotty nappy hair. I needed discourse not antagonisms, intellectual rage, not armed struggle, dialogue not wars, talking with not talking to. She was saying seek and find an alternative to this historically bitter factional rivalry and tribalism gripping humanity in politics and religion. Often, she would remind me that the Samaritan did not know the victim of robbers beatings. He did not know his religious or political affiliation neither did he see the color of his skin. He saw a wounded suffering human being needing help, and blood, blood like eyes fire, had no race. I understand my Father precisely now, when he would say people are people everywhere -- the interpretation coming by way of Mama's outreach. Sound wisdom? When you listen to its sound, Mama is a sort of wisdom body universally, you know. Mama implies feeding, sustenance, protection, even lessons in interdependence, interconnectedness. Our brother Ernest has informed me that Mama always warned him to save his money in order to build his house. Our youngest brother Albert reminded me of one of Mama's frequent remarks: you cannot kiss your own elbow. There are scratching spots on my back my fingers cannot immediately reach. Yoga abandoned? Would be careless of me to deny this African tradition. Didn't know eh. Her acrobatics legacy was in truth, largely spiritual. However I understood her meticulous observations of interdependence, more so, interconnectedness. It is still basic to political economy, is it not? It is still the business of communion and community. It is still basic to trade and barter where it exists. It is at the heart of women pooling monies and paying each the lump sum every two or three weeks. Such fiscal practices thrive in good measure among Caribbean and Third World women, but certainly not in large measure as it used to. Politics and religion have attempted to divide West Indian and world societies and yet their communities, their localisms remain dominant forces interpellating breath's true democracy, life's real economy. Who can doubt that many times they were tired, many times their efforts at survival frustrated. Who can deny that they found refuge in religion. Who was it who said religion is the sigh of the oppressed creature, the heart of a heartless world? St. Paul understood the partial view religion permitted and the Rabbi himself took on the more magnificent and spiritually abundant view when he with absolute authority and power stated: I am the way the truth and the life! He could have been responding to the question who is I Am, except he went on to say that no one comes to the Father except by way of who or what he is. She believed this to be the way. In her world there was no other, not even a she, maybe, except Mary, and she was the Mother, though in her Catholic faith they referred to her as the Mother of God. Were they confusing hierarchies? If God has a Mother, then they're pretty close to the cosmic consciousness brewing in Hinduism. Or were they saying that Jesus is God? Then, who was the Mother of the Holy Spirit? Mary? Wooo! And who was Mary? A Middle Eastern woman whom so much or all of Europe and Latin America came to worship? Was she African or even Black? Say what you want -- the Mother of the Son of God for whom a body was prepared in Heaven, has to be special in the universal scheme of things. Could I say the same for the Mother of Buddha, Socrates, Mohammed, Krishna, Lao Tzu, Gandhi, Plato, King, Mother Theresa, Lady Diana, Maharishi, Bob Marley, Harriet Tubman, Marcus Garvey, Nelson Mandela? Or should I settle for Peter, Paul and Mary? Mama, was I pushing it?

Truth is, she was not conservative neither was she insular. In my late teens, one of our home-town leftists gave me a booklet on dialectical materialism and she stormed at me. What was it about Marxist-Leninist thought that my Mother knew in 1974. I never saw the booklet again. Around that same year I bought a copy of the soundtrack to the film "Jesus Christ Superstar." I was a teacher then investing in music, books of the wickedest (not evil) variety. In the scene out of Gethsemane, Jesus says to his Father to act quickly before he changed his mind. My Mother asked me "what kind of record is that?" She suggested that I get rid of it. I hid it. She did not mind the European classics from Chopin, Frantz, Berlioz, Tchaikovsky and Beethoven, not to mention Wagner. Generally, they did not lyricize. I found them in the hold of a Swedish haul captained by my brother-in-law. Evidently they were not as overt as Superstar's music composer Andrew Lloyd Webber and its lyricist Tim Rice, neither were they as anarchic as those early European music dialecticians. Overt.

In those times, Jimmy Cliff's "Vietnam" elicited a pensive moment. Listening to him sing the same song today and in light of the Iraq, Afghan or Syrian conflict I am assured of virtues in honest story-telling. In the song "Vietnam," A soldier writes home, saying that he will be home soon, his time will be up "some time in June." Which June? From that same LP -- and it was long-playing in those days -- my Mother enjoyed Cliff's "Many Rivers To Cross" and "Wonderful World Beautiful People." Apparently these lyrics, unlike those in Rice's Superstar, did not to her, entail overt expressions of religious and political radicalism, but threw thought into wise and I dare say reasoned reflection. I loved the track "My Ancestors" which I played over and over again. There was something assured in the lines: "my ancestors they were mighty men/and my son/he will be one of them/ and they'll just look at him." They fired my teenage mind -- I needed to find those ancestors, to know them, those mighty people.

I don't believe she heard Cliff later in the 80s when he became a Muslim singing: "stand up and fight back/you have nothing to lose," echoing her call to her children. She might not have heard him sing "Bongo Man," warning that "if you follow politicians/you will never come at all...and if you follow heads of churches/you will never come at all/we are going to Zion." Its essence bubbled in her. She prayed lifting her eyes to the hills -- Zion -- from where she sought spiritual support, evidences of sight recovery and yes, economic ease in the manner that God works best to favour his people. Cliff was heading to Zion. She knew that place. This was the abode of Rastafarians, a holy place, a place of trembling -- Dread in the presence of Fire. She, a daughter of Zion, lifted her eyes to Zion. There, to the Rastafarians, was where Jah/God lived. She looked to that Zion for help. She received help, not sight in the same way like the man who cried out for mercy from Jesus, the Son of David. Hers must have been inner vision, power of discernment. In response to the Man's cry, Jesus practiced medicine, this time as an ophthalmologist. He was addressed by the Man as the Son of the King who wrote and sang Psalms accompanied by a harp, psalter or other stringed instrument. Probably she needed musical accompaniment to have the Kingdom come, to experience bliss, utter joy in sight recovery. I would hear that woman chant Psalms day after day out of the depth. Something is supposed to move down there. I mean, a drifting algae, a primitive cell, bits of tentacles, sounds of a whale's harmonics, Jonah's embodiment remembrances rippling subatomically, cognitive tremors of his Mother's reflections on his exile in a mammal's gut, an absolutely beautiful coral reef ecosystem, a rising underwater volcano, a seventy-five billion dollar submarine, something. At the very least she could've felt warm trickles of hormonal information passed on from her Mother in her utero fays reconstituting her genetics, strengthening her primary particles. You know, something out of the depth.

It is this feeling of her presence that engages my thought and warms my imagination this New York morning. It is this knowing an accompanying yet invisible liquid energy walking with me. There was a place in her where we her children, rested at conception. We fed from her feeding, drank her emotions. As we grew she grew. As she changed we changed. When she died something in us died. Something in us opened up a door to emotions -- a child's cry in an adult's body. Our birthing could have resulted in her death, so too could her death during delivery have resulted in our death.

What is this. Wait. Ancient utterances are trickling into this text. Embryonic communication? Wait. Listen.

I died in victory my Son. I died in Christ. Don't hesitate to write this. This is whom I believe in. It is Jesus Christ I trusted, the one you learned about when I sent you to Sunday School, the anointed one you sang about each Sunday before going to matinee. You should know that my redeemer lives. What joy, what blessed joy I find in this assurance. I hope you understand. There was a moment while dying when I felt I had won. I had fought the good fight gained a good report. Hold fast and strong to the knowledge of God in Christ Jesus. You too will feel the peace I felt on departure assured that we shall all meet on that beautiful shore. O Mama. How those redemption songs could be converted into weapons of spiritual warfare from their opiate functions to instruments of rebellion and revolt. Indeed, resurrection is a spiritual revolution!

CHAPTER 4

My Mother's Kind

She died with glaucoma. Were that glaucoma had died with her! She had prayed each day to the Lord, her light, her salvation. It seemed that that light was apart from the body though in it. Was she kept physically blind in order to walk not by sight but by way of the Lord? This is indeed a remarkable way of developing trust in the midst of a grand disconnect, the first part of the untold story. There is, among our people of African descent in the Caribbean, an unexplained gap between the spiritual and physical. In West Indian history, flesh was to be denied except as source of reproduction, sex and labor. Spirit was with God and God was in Heaven. Heaven in the context of exploited labor, was apparently not in body. This was not a relationship between a river, streams and tributaries, vine and branches. Those earthly lords believed that spirit did not flow into mind and mind into body. I gather slavery was white spirit business -- not coming down, not condescending to Black chattel.

Our God will keep them chained, those masters proclaim over dinner and wine. God will keep them ignorant in our favor. Whatever changes are to take place must take place without the congregation knowing. The chemistry and electricity of a Sunday morning August 1 service must not be made explicit.

Tell you, in this mode of return, I hear those old vampires voices cursing, saying those men and women of color flow thought with speech too readily. They may begin to think that "Almighty God is a living man" and we do not want them to assume such authority. Next moment they will want to extend such power into economic zones or culture interests in self-determination.

You have to believe exploiters were that deliberate. That too, our Mothers and Fathers of the time had to deal with. They did not openly call such wicked thought, repression, suppression or evil -- maybe some thought it to be the works of Satan, while others even perceived it as someone in and around their community trying to hold them back. The matter of suppression had trickled right down the line, down those steep economic slides, and my people, my people in their gracefulness, described circumstances surrounding economic exploitation, as the will of God. What a strange interpretation. In the mode of sound resistance, they literally counted their blessings whether they be food on the table, a gift from an overseas child, cash in hand or health, pure health. Truly, there came times too, when they could wait no more. Thing is, in spite of their capacity to overcome, reward for too many of my Mother's generation was in the hereafter. That ethic, pervasive as it was, subconsciously as it was buried, hindered over time, the complete expression of an entrepreneurial spirit. Yet, much to their credit, much to their resilience, they surfaced to feed and sustain themselves, their children and communities. Just imagine what they could have done. Those who oppress, suppress, repress do not know the needle. Most non-prescribed actions that would enhance our people's material and physical well-being were classified as sin, and actually accompanied by the most horrendous forms of punishment and fear-installation techniques. Philosophy too was tucked away in proverbial sayings that remained stunted, guilt-laden, resistant to fresh interpretation. In the case of glaucoma, she prayed that this thorn be taken away. But interpretively religiously, the thorn was supposed to prevent one from being too puffed up. St. Paul, who understood powerfully what constituted a critical practice, an impaired eye, would probably think me malicious in saying that as long as you're a partial in these times, it's good for business. At any rate she did a courageously Pauline deed: in spite of glaucoma and its damaging experience she held on to her faith. The problem existed but it, it was no longer a barrier. It figures requiring a depth-psychology switching system. Psychology? That mid-ground architecture in motion was wild habitat, this neck simply bridging. This middle passage, this psychoscape between spirit and body, apparently did not connect in the slave body. Those who invented splitting personalities were convincing themselves of that error ceaselessly. This eco-knowledge around us -- the one we thought of as it thought us -- was not our property, they said. It's surreal, others shouted angrily spitting. It does not exist; those things you people think. Who can prove it? Tell you, my Mother's kind muttered, it's my property, though you surround, hate, racialize communities, control landed rights. Private property? Sleep was theirs, wasn't it? Whose dreams did they dream when rivers flooded and full moons lifted oceans? Whose dreams did they dream when each born child was fed? In their world and yours, sleep was good for refreshing. Later in your world dreams raced in Freuds individual domain, fearful of deep drops into this uncontrollable valley of desolation -- equating patriarchy with melting stone, iron, steel, molten lava. Using the mind? Forget about that. Use the brain, they shouted, the arithmetical one. This you must've learned by way of their curriculum. But thinking for yourself? Keep your eyes on the Lord. He will provide from Heaven. Even while this thought homicide raged, God moved in liquid energy spaces in their thoughts. Could they know? If only they opened their mouths. Mama, vowing to be obedient sang, "keep your eyes on Jesus." She must've died in Christ. In her living days she was convinced that not even death could separate her from that love of God manifested in and shining out from Jesus, the Anointed One. This is not archaeology. The crumbling brain, a withering hypothalamus, sapping of the lobes, disappearance of corneas and sockets painlessly -- those are of interest to scholars, forensic experts. To die in Christ is another. Wait. Silence! She speaks!

This is part of the process my Son. You give up the flesh. I was fed that I might feed the Earth; Those who would come from me and those who are to come from it. I am Mother. Earth is Mother also. I am fed by what I return to. We are no different. You are my male child and yet different from me your female Mother. You are no different from the Earth. It absorbs me so easily, indeed, I am not hurt by the crawl of a worm through my heart nor the gathering of dirt in my mouth nor the softening of my muscle as flesh returns to flesh and its ancient substance. I no longer live in twenty-four hour frames of a Sun-God. Darkness and light come from the same place and do not punctuate my utterances in words or in flesh now singing the absorption song. Mental arithmetic I did as a timekeeper is now counted as spirit of grace. Where I go now eighty-one years is a grain a seed a speck in the House of the Mother of God, the land of the master archaeologist. Here, they uncover wisdom that will not be measured in weight depth. Here glaucoma is nothing, illusion is made real, partialities made whole. Those fingers that touched you, now move in unison with a rush of wind or thunderous hurricane. My heart is nowhere arrested in time and erotica. No one uses me and I use no one. In truth there is no reason. Sounds like a fairy tale?

There is so much hunger, poverty, loneliness and disease under the sun. You have to see it from here.

What if I told you Earth longs to absorb us with the same eagerness that it wants to feed us. This should not sound cruel. There is no inequality here -- the wisdom field of non-discrimination reigns here. Indeed I am subject and equal to all living things in and under the soil, sun.

Rain come soaking through, wets my peach dress and stockings, fills my bed with water and tries to float me. Fortunately I am in structures that do not function to any corporate time and logic. Structures? Didn't know eh? Didn't know that Spirit has form, an anatomy some contend. Though a child may be born deformed, this same child is not born a fish. Special needs? Honest, why should a Mother abandon her children or child. when it's all done the sacrifice would be worthy. No woman should leave her children hungry. Just a moment. I feel the body giving its sexuality in exchange for children's food sleep and schooling. I feel symbiotic pulls of umbilical cords. I feel passion recalled. She is paid and buys quality oils. She anoints her own her salvation. She gives thanks in tears. It is an ecstasy. Her children are fed her anger released. Her breasts are ravaged yet feed those who come after with a milk of kindness and love untouched, untamed by the fingers, teeth, tongues, lips and hissings of men. Beyond all male control, male entry, lives a spirit stable assured that, her hungry must be fed.

Organs are frozen now. There is darkness here. There's light here. I do not need to physically see. I am now spectacle visible to all, see all. I do not hear recrimination nor does it matter that a hand is stretched against my little ones. They're fighters with many eyes. Those who ever hated me or my offspring come out to play. The mystery interpreter is no longer here. The calm know-it-all Mama, the protector is gone forever, they claim. Little do they understand Spirit of the Living God. But I want you to enjoy yourself. Don't be burdened by too much heavy thought and thinking. Laugh. Run. Dance, Eat, dress colorfully, live with and in water, Waitukubuli's many rivers.

Love? Oh yes I fell in love. I had desires too and passionate ones. There were days when being in love was all that mattered. That genre of love made me happy and happiness has a way of feeding us. I knew those who eat better in the presence of their lover. I knew those who did not care what time it was, or who did not even feel hunger or the pass of time. Yes I was in love. As I grew older I realized the course of life, recognized its turns and ups. People lived off each other. Just imagine me speaking with your Father. What comes out of my mouth is treated as gospel and I think the same about his. We had frequent arguments though. I was strong-headed and he was a rebel. We did not last much longer after your birth. But I could not keep you away from him. This is why in the years before you went to high-school and sea as a teenager I would send you to holiday with your aunt only to see him and he to see you. It was difficult not to have seen someone for thirty years, someone I once cared about. We met in between but very briefly. I always thought he would've lived a few more years. He died before me. He was such a brilliant man but somehow I believe he wasted his life. I did not dislike what I saw in you: I was concerned about where it would lead. We are both gone now. The body he yearned for is now Earths'. He is also Earths'.

Tell you. It is good for a man to understand the role of his Father. He is spiritual guide. I am protector. Spirit of the living God is both plus. Quantum. A man should not turn his Son away from his Mother neither should a woman turn her Son away from his Father especially when both parents have brothers and sisters and the child, though he or she may not receive the love of either parent, can be loved by an uncle or aunt. A married Mother should not turn her children away from their brothers and sisters born of another woman. Those from the outside may be even better sons and daughters than those within. Let the turning away be a matter of his or her choosing. Life has a way of playing an opposite game. Sometimes the child has to reject the parents thus causing them to be better persons. They should however reconcile their differences at some point, some say before death.

It is also true that except when born with some serious defect, children have a way of surviving. In your time it was easier, not only because parents did not reject their children, neither was it on account of the plentifulness of food shared within the clan. I believe people cared and this positively affected a Mother's health. She spoke truth!

I can say we boys and girls consumed anything edible growing around us long before food became fast. I remember when cattle produced true milk and beef, and most physical disorders were external. Thank God they surfaced. Our society had not yet metamorphosized into one of the living dead, into what Pope John Paul Second referred to as a culture of death!

CHAPTER 5

Our Mother's Insight

She had eight of us four boys and four girls. Five were by one father two by another and I, the only one she had by my Father. She and her extended family, fathered each and gave to all the salt of the Earth. Was this why she died or became blind? What is it about sex that centralizes it in the Christian world of sin? Why sex? Am I forgetting greed, envy, hate, lusts, idolatry, covetousness, stealing, warring. Indeed Mama, all have sinned.

I think of these women whose only war was with daily life, everyday living. I shudder sometimes when I see their physical end. Was it because they worked too hard, did not maintain a proper diet, whatever this is. Was it because they did not exercise? Were they too free sexually, having their children by different men? Was salvation for the married woman and condemnation for the unwed. What of the barren and those with souls like Lady Diana? What of those who cultured their children with the heart of a Mother Teresa, or the Mother of God along the Milky Way to register for the census, and yet another -- between the slave-woman and man, that child who became the liberator? Cultivating children?

Wash your face. Comb your hair. Brush your teeth. Lift your feet when walking. Don't drag them. Get ready to go to church. Remember the Creator in the days of your youth. Pray. Don't talk too much. Don't eat from anyone. Greet relatives and older people. Be neat. Be punctual. Be consistent particularly in your work. Whenever you get back from church put your clothes away. A single Mother's dreams?

My children, if I had the chance to I would live over again. It is good to live. When you attended the funeral you felt strong and encouraged. This is also good. There is no pain here. I am in the Earth and the Earth is in me. When it bursts like a violent volcano I burst. Like the river I run and like the Ocean I rise and fall. The volcano does not belong to the Red races and the ocean to the White, neither do the rivers to the Black. My body slips into, sleeps above roots of trees buried before I was born long before Columbus rested his eyes and head on this land and discovered himself, discovered the land's divine capacity to heal his defeats. Soon roots will wind through me sucking poisons at the knots in my liver. Wrapping me enfolding me is substance to which I am equal in age and time and yet we barely know it. What is in me is as old as the Earth, the living Earth. My child, the truth is we as human beings, as inhabitants in this living space, feel loss. When the oceans swallowed your sister my laughter was taken too. In my mind I journeyed down those dark unfathomable caverns no steps no footholds no platforms. I followed her trying to remember whether there was a time as a baby when she kicked in the womb and I did not notice. She must have tried to stand out of fear in a bottomless place crisscrossed by the Atlantic and Caribbean seas. I grieved her tragic disappearance and non-discovery -- the fact that her body never came back to us. Deep secrets in the dark they call it. God knows. My son, your brother died in a London hospital. I heard his voice call out to me as a baby, days before I was told about it. No wonder when the news came to me that he was sick I said just tell me he is dead. I knew you all, the remaining six, wanted to protect me from the impact but I had already been informed. A child cannot be hidden from its Mother's spirit even its Mother's intuition. I feel my children, could look into their eyes and see anything inside. Even in the years when I could not see, I heard distinctions in voices and could identify the slightest nuances. Mother's love goes beyond possession. Mothers know simultaneous pain and pleasure, gifts in separation. I had to cut you away from me that you might continue living. I would've cut you off myself if I had to; a practice not anathema to our history of women in the Caribbean. I do not know how much you know about the spirit thinking and actions of the Caribbean's Warrior Woman. Pity those who possess their children holding them prisoner in the name of love. I did not keep you. Rather, I let you go gently slow, sometimes vigorously robustly with strength and confidence rooted in a profound faith swifter than your steps or speech gait and look. What I saw pleased me. What I did not see pleased me even more. Every now and then I would witness that fire in your sisters in your brothers that energy to do more than just survive. You know we've been told so much about the heart. It's time to use your heads too. A few years from now you will find my remains: skeleton and no flesh. You'll not find many teeth if any. My eyes ears tongue nostrils will not be there. You will find a frame and the bones to my fingers. You will find no muscle no memory no words no smiles. There will be no heartbeat no pulse no form for doctors to gaze at. The involuntary would truly have gone to its essence. There will be no slim or obese figure no there will be no digestion no gastric juices no villi no trabecular meshwork. There will be no Schlemm's chamber no retina no macular no vessels no ships bearing blood to the eye's horizon. There will be no fussy spirit no vexatious soul no anger no pancreas no spleen. Makes you muse, when you think about body-parts given attention in modern cultures. Details systematically internalized in biology are superficial here -- initial media to this greater more indelible calligraphy. Yet, in the face of this wasting away, this dissipation, laughingly, I continue to believe that it was this milk I drank as a child. You wouldn't believe, but those progressively hard fingernails would be gone, clipped over and over by shifting microbes. In this world of the dead, ancestors receive newcomers. I was received by children at one gate. There are ancestors too. Let me not disturb your patriarchal socialization. I am not a scientist of society, neither am I one of the body and its transformation. We are spirits here.

CHAPTER 6

Here without Apology

A woman is struggling with a visual impairment and believes that through prayer and medicines her disorder can be cured. She is confident that her God the God of Abraham Isaac and Jacob will never fail her. She said it each day: he will never leave you nor forsake you. What she does not know is that the beta-blockers, the eye-drops will fail her. What she does not know is that the return of elevated intraocular pressure cannot be abated through the use of Diamox and Pilocarpine. She does not know that Medicine as practiced today, only treats; it no longer cures and those who have been trained to diagnose and treat believe also in God to whom they pray, on whom they depend for wise decision, a sound judgement. They too are in search of healing, in search of remembering. She knows that her grand-aunt was visually impaired. To her the peripheral loss is not linked to nutrition deficiency, neither is it to a trace of diabetes in the family. You know, this 1920s woman would finally rule out the gene thing. I mean, from her pelvis, her thighs to her very soles, she walked like a soldier dressed in armor of light. Yet, tender optic nerve fibers continued to be damaged, the ophthalmologists observed. Acupuncturists might've identified meridian points to the liver along the inner length of her left leg above the ankle; feet did not disconnect eyes. In our home practice, in much of western practice, the connect had not been made. A bridge was needed between the two communities of prayer and medicines, prayer and body. There are those who would argue that were it not for the medicines she would have gone blind before seventy. There are also those who would say categorically that prayer gave her strength to stay seeing. We need those who pray, meditate, argue for percolation of faith energy into the affected tissue. We need those who are not guessers, who do not pander to the pharmaceutical industry, yet know how, and are zealous advocates for sight restoration, especially when they know it can be done and is being done albeit for those who can pay.

With holy violence, we need breathe in a formula of Love, electrifying dendrites. Mind shifting, impacting cell's synapses? Yes. Surely it could've been cultured, and I believe they nurtured unconsciously, a culture of healing psychosoma with its many scars. Those scars served as vehicles to healing practice. In silence they dwelt on flesh's skin knitting cell, patient thought over healing courses. Those strategic warriors needed to know psycho-soma's field, its spirit. Indeed, too many of their subtler thoughts were not about production of sugar, tobacco, cotton, bananas. There was an element awakening in this highly prized soma. Didn't have to learn what we had always known to master. They took to hoping. Simple? Do not underestimate hopes and aspirations of a people who've been systemically oppressed. Hopes become realities in hearts, minds and souls of another generation.

From the days of her fiftieth birthday till her death at eighty-one she kept hope alive. But visual impairment it seemed, was a story already written by molten fingers. Despite its formlessness, she knew from time as we say, this spirit of hope, its transcendent wing, its pure flexibility, its memory. She knew hope was not in a cask or measured in tonnages. Spirit of sacrifice? In her gracefulness, this woman had courage to count blindness as trial. She saw an overcoming but it was not for her to realize in her body. This is a significant West Indian historical issue.

Finiteness of human flesh will forever baffle younger Caribbean and world generations. As yet, they do not understand why a body grows weak, hurts, (dis)integrates, dies. When younger, their bodies, temples of the Holy Spirit are so strong so full of energy. They are not yet aware that this energy comes from that Holy Spirit! They feel such sense of joy under this tent. They experience love at the very least a taste of the real and wish sometimes that time and the full moon could stand still. It is beauty, glimpses of its form, its truth-place in the Heavens. Is it any wonder they think immortality? Isn't this results of dreams, hopes? Its evidence is in us West Indians. I think spirit of immortality is in all peoples; I just stand for my people whose bodies were criminalized by the millions, whose story sprouts against all odds. From where we stand, dead seeds are bursting, breaking with disturbing silence. Science? I have heard the scientists speak about eugenics and the works of James Watson and hear them tongue-tied on the subject of values and ethics. To what end is that knowledge being sought? They are forced by dint of its history to revert to stories of the Third Reich a super race a more intelligent child a stronger athlete and the futile debate surrounding color of eyes. Immortality flashes. Longevity rumbles into, passed nitrogen atoms. Silence listens to those who'd rather speak murmuringly about earthworms than Christ, those finding the latter boring, unscientific. Translation of the Christ-life into science is near impossible for them. There is no biology no zoology here. The eternal spirit within the human body will not be reduced to the microscopic. Death is the problem. While they understand seeds germinative process by way of dying, in the case of the human, they seem to want to eliminate the transformation, the transition, the going-over, or should I say, the going into the heart of Life. Persons with disabilities do not have a place in their world. The poor and afflicted will not survive a day. The Bible, the same Bible, the IMF and the World Bank give people in the Third World three score and ten. The DNA protagonists say they would settle for one hundred and twenty. They are not under the yoke of the New Hampshire institutions neither do they care about the saying that Jesus Christ is the first born of the dead. They are comfortable some of them. I believe however that there is some concern for healing struggling with a supremacy ideology.

Memory reveals memory and darkness is not steel. God knows what is hidden. Stem cell research draws its healing cluster from the patient to regenerate growth; in the case of the visually impaired, ophthalmologists envisage rebirth of the optic nerve. This phenomenal finding is not in the bones of one race. The patient's ability to cure is in the patient. This probably makes restoration more difficult in a western world where the within is still restricted and even taboo. We are so far gone in the material world that unfortunately it is just as difficult coming back as it is going ahead. We choose the latter, its plethora of divisions and classifications. Love they say, is unerotic here even as compassion defeats the purpose of correct social and natural science. Just imagine scientists placating anger, or separating joy and pain or even eliminating strains felt in the woman's knees when rains are three days away. They would love to keep for the pharmaceutical industry, knowledge of the balance of the moon and menstrual cycle. Mama, is this death story running into overload, shattering text and context?

African-American writer James Baldwin, once observed that to act is to be committed and to be committed is to be in danger. This narrative course has brought me face to face with danger. I have known crude beginnings. I have known vague. I have come into, upon this place learning, learning to be brave, learning that I had set my hand to the plough -- apparently along where Nobel-laureate in Literature, St. Lucian Derek Walcott hailed as the straits of Heaven. I was going to be lost at times and I wonder now if I should call it lost or searching. I only have to connect whether from the deep to heights, the lowly to the elevated and lifted-up darkness into light, the prostitute's white linen to the puritan's frock the priest to the clinical hypnotherapist, the fisherman to the royal housekeeper wherever they figured along these straits each bearing their goblet, each carrying the mark of the wild in the flesh, its provocations, its syndromes its commanding trumpet-calls to discipline its frailties its passionate spaces, their contribution to thought and its gathering up in reason demanding that brothers and sisters dwell together in unison, with oil blessings and thanksgivings. Here we do not bear the mark of separation between secular and sacred, an embodiment we should not deny. It is liberated people's sacrifice of joy, a contextualizing of our material economic reality. This is the point when thought and imagination shango. It is here that I want to sleep but sleeping only wakes me. It is here that flesh is weak and the spirit shakes dust off its wings. Here food is media, drink a rendezvous with rivers. Fish is now sky-life and corn the wind-shaken blade. It is here in this dance that the musician's finger-tips feel like marble on the strings sliding, picking with assurance. Thanks to Dominican musician Maximin Powell for this insight. Hail Bro! Here in the geography of mind and soul, time and space have no boundaries and physics earns a quantum quality. Here is a flawless acupunctural contact a Hindu's bliss a Buddha's heavy stillness a Christian's resurrection rumbling, yes, a Rastafarian's fire I blazing into Babylon's evil. Here in the invisible wind is a transformation at Mecca, a humanist's urge to love an atheist in the heights of reason. Here is a Quaker in silence. Here is a Baptist in the throes of the spirit, a pentecostalist's ascension into passion of prayer, a fisherman's full net bursting in morning's Sun, a Kabbalist silenced, a blind man cured a Mother's gift of a child after three days into labor. It is the oneness plane. Here the milk knows the child and the blood its bone. Here the prey knows its hunter and the whale communes with the language and structure of the oceans governments. It is here that the congregation mediates and priests follow. Here the ant marries the Internet and they build an institution of undeclared ownership. It is no one's property -- it will not be taken colony. Here men cannot legitimize self-interest or vagabonds reject love for justice. Here there is no insecurity in neighborhoods and mushroom clouds will not eat the lungs nor weaken bodies to insanity. Blessed are those who have evidence of this here. It is crucial, since here too, deception thrives on restless minds. It appears that anything that can be thought of already exist. There is no need for thought. All one has to do is taste, consume. Truly they satisfy your every need. Think of it they say. It is available. Here thought is material expression, reflection flighty. Prayer takes time and time is money. It is here some claim that history is dead and men in their reach for unlimited wealth in the face of poverty, death hunger and desperation, disease and control contend that God too is dead. It is here they conclude that spirit ends and the dollar begins. It is here that the righteous are persecuted and the Middle Passage rolls. It is here that tens, hundreds, thousands of skeletal remains are scattered on ocean floors. See a Mother and her child rising from the ocean floor, yet another and still another -- this one clutching a Coptic-looking cross. This one died in rough seas jumping the deck. These stories?

I have only just arrived. My colors are fresh and dripping. Here I learn. Here every entrant learns. In fact, here we eat and learn. We consume the Word. We are sure that before the thing was one sound, one verse, the Word becoming!

I am aware that I am writing about my Mother's passing, recording thoughts I have of her as I reflect on the things we used to talk about and the type of person I knew. I cannot be exact about her thoughts, not even when I have her direct words. But I take the chance to extend on issues we discussed during her life and the period when she was more acutely blind. With some rigor, based on the endless exchanges of meanings we shared and the character of the person I grew to know, I reflect on ideas she might have had which she partially expressed, thoughts she might have wanted to express but did not think them timely and, what she might have wanted to say but did not have the time. I take the opportunity to extend her thoughts, sayings, songs and quotes into my thoughts -- a sort of cross-germination. I do something that may be considered unorthodox: I think of her as living where she is. From there she speaks. In the process I am extended to places I've never been and seen -- into fields of thoughts I wrestle with. This makes for a wonderful challenge -- thoughts calling out for exhaustive treatment. She too, might be amazed by the substance I find in her simple life. Invariably, my own experience, my ideas wheel is turning on this matter without apology; even when I find playful rescue and succor in matters of the spirit and the resurrection, I do not want to be vulgar about this liberation this salvation. It is here that my Mother would have expected the greatest care to be given to the subject.

As in what follows, I chart from traces and bits, a communication out of my mourning. It is gentle, communicative tissue, so tender I hear rendezvous. I hear, take time to know. I will visit again soon. I hear, possibly out of divine communication, remind me to tell you about Jesus Christ. This dying on the cross for our sins is so simple and yet still mysterious I reckon. I wonder if there is real interest where you are, in the crucified Christ and his resurrection. We'll find out when we communicate next time.

That was lightning confirming the communication one time. Lightning? Forgive me. I am Caribbean. by one time I mean instantly. Time is zero here. Next time is zero one. There is a playfulness about communication, music and mathematics. Instant? Just think of this: the spirit of God hovers over the waters -- three quarters of the human body. Even if you don't believe this aqua picture, this event of a spirit over Earth's Waters, isn't this a moment in time and eternity. Spirit on water? This is indeed, Holy Water. This is dramatic. Imagine silence communicating down to the very cell transmitting, broadcasting! There is light, a planet's ring blinking, a floodlight. Got to play like early Life. Noah is not yet in the area, in the hood, in the time zone. See what happens: the narrative is eager to surface.

Identify the here and now, logic screams. State your specificity. Which city? Specifi? On this plane of life all are revealed. No one runs a hidden story nor holds intentions which the law will not attempt to unravel. Surface from Specifi, they shout. Tell us where on West Indian plantation society you saw treadmills breaking women's shins, women's tibias in plantation yards. Men suffered under aroma of the acacia tree, I answered softly. Still. historian Philip Sherlock I added for clarification, skillfully juxtaposes fragrances with an appalling magistracy between 1834 and 1838. Even churches were burnt; their crosses turned to ashes, no food for microbes. Spirit on water? Let's play skip.

Welcome to the text of slime. They want you to surface. They want you to surface from a narrative celebrating my passing and your textual Lexus rolls into a plantation yard! Wow! As my womb is consumed in Fire of Earth my children are spirited.

As she returns again, sense of history warms my head. It's about the past, great events and people. It's about crisis -- an opportunity for change. It is truly about what is happening now. As her stomach is consumed her tongue melts. I remember her fluency, chanting her dwelling in the secret place of the Most High, her love for good soup and speech. "I will say of the Lord, he is my refuge and my strength; in him will I trust." When she stepped out of her house she was thereby armed: "Lord you are my strength." It was a daily ascendancy.

Each day she traveled to work for England's Geest Industries reflecting on the intricate operations of such a trans-national entity. Geest fed her family; her labor kept our family alive. My people remain exploited to this day, the ones who set out each day to their banana fields praying Psalms. Geest would pack up and leave, having maximized its profits (though a few do not think so) ending an era of industry and the practice of a particular kind of horticulture and faith.

She saw and weighed trucks and loads of trucks rolling on to scales and into plants where they were offloaded -- their bananas wrapped, carried and carefully placed in lighters, then towed by tugs to ships -- white, tall floating objects awaiting hundreds of women carriers running with a bunch on their heads to those lighters tied on the jetty's side. They ran a full hundred yards or more, forming a line for those going out and another for those coming back to sheds. Some carried even while a few months pregnant. A few developed a reputation for speed: it was only natural. They formed a crucial link in the division of labor, the chain between the ready-to-ship product and its loading. They would later be replaced by conveyor belts. Mama worked as operator of the huge scales, in accounts, and with responsibility for the company's storeroom. You should have seen her, standing from morning to midnight with a break for lunch and supper. You should have seen her disciplined body behind this machine sliding its weights after the truck and its load had taken up position on the steel platform. You should have seen her balance gross and tare weights, measuring the slightest tilt, hands light, wonder in her young eyes. Mama worked diligently at the scales. In her thirty-five years, never was there a report of underweighing anyone. Never was there a report of goods, materials such as nails, paint, bolts, coils of rope or anything missing or unaccounted for. Never did a carrier-woman say she was short-paid. As destiny would have it, a truck-driver and excellent mechanic would become father to five of her children. Think of how proud he was of her as she weighed his truck and hundreds, indeed, thousands of others. She worked diligently till the end, till retirement knowing that even van Geest had a master. Did he and his corporate executives die in Christ? Did Christ Jesus die for his sins. Could this be another "amazing grace" story?

CHAPTER 7

The Blessing

I felt a simple cry when my brother called from Miami to say Mama is dead. I had last seen her in May 2003 when I returned to Dominica for the launching of a television documentary I had produced and directed on behalf of UNICEF, Christian Children's Fund and the Caribbean Support Initiative/Bernard van Leer Foundation. No matter where I was in this world I would have found my way home. This was the end of an era of experience and the beginning of another. We who had only been in New York for eight months, had very little money and I was the only one who could travel. When I decided on my departure date, Albert, the last of Mama's eight living in Miami, paid two-thirds of the fare. Thankfully. Truly the wife and children were hurt by the passing and they would've loved to be in Dominica for the funeral. We marked the few hours after the news with an incomprehensible silence -- Dominica in May and Dominica again in August. In May I celebrated launching of a film, in August I marked, mourned a death.

The fact that we had spoken all my life compared with her utter silence over the seven-day period I spent in Dominica in May signaled an ominous change: she had begun her exit. That silence! This was my Mother and this was not my Mother. This must be her before she gave birth to me. No, this is her speaking a language I did not speak. A conflict must be resolving itself. Another fecund force had taken her hand and attention. She answered me only when I addressed her as Miss Daisy. She did not respond to the call Ma! She sat upright and looked with blind eyes straight at me almost majestically carrying a simple yet complete smile. After a while I no longer expected her to speak. I spoke. I told her the wife and children were well. This, she always asked about whenever I would visit while in Dominica. I told her I missed her, loved her, and always will. In spite of what I had just said, I kept feeling I had not said enough and when I spoke she seemed after a while to lose interest. She was on the run and, I was only one of the persons in her life-scape now. I either had to catch up with her or leave the race and when I thought I did I felt like an insignificant runner. I kept thinking that she might be showing me, showing me what she wanted me to do or be after she was gone or after I had left Dominica. Imagine that thought, creative, trying to grasp meaning in the actions of a dying Mother. She wanted me to be silent. In truth I needed to taste true quality and power in silences. What did Kahlil Gibran say in "The Broken Wings" touching what is greater and purer than what the mouth utters? "Silence," Gibran counsels, "illuminates souls. Silence whispers to hearts and brings souls and hearts together."

In May while sitting at her bedside in this field of silence, I placed my right hand on her leg. I would usually massage her shoulders, her upper and lower back, the muscles in her legs and have her apply a pressure against mine on her toes. She had to push them out while I pushed in. I always wanted to see the extent to which her neuromuscular system was connecting. Her head and feet showed marvelous communication yet her eyes were in disorder. I soothed her leg along the lines of the tibia.

This time she was in pain and moaning softly. However it seemed more emotional than physical. I had not touched her in a long time and she knew my fingers were strong though she often complained that my hands were too soft. I took to massaging her soles up to her knees by way of the gastrocnemius or what we Dominicans, call gwabjamb.

She would always let me do that. Suddenly, she took my left hand in hers and began squeezing it with penetrating force from her hard fingernails. It became painful and she seemed to insist that I allow her to continue. I set up a resistance in my fingers as she applied force. This struggle in the hands and fingers went on for about five minutes. I realized that this was not about she being punitive. What was she communicating after three days of intense silence? Her action was one of putting something in and into my hand. She held my left palm down firmly with her left hand holding at my wrist. She would then extend her right hand out, as if taking something from thin air and pressing it into my left palm pinned down on her bed. The force came from her shoulders down to her finger-tips. Even when I resisted she insisted: she was going to press it in anyway. My palm and fingers were flesh and bones feeling pain but I had to be tougher. When she sensed that the pain was unbearable she pushed my hands away. My daughter Glendora told me lovingly, "that was when she did not like you." There must have been such a time in our lives. An older woman told me she was giving me the blessing. The blessing? What a revelation to my body's resisting. This event was preceded and followed by silence.

Three months later, she would die, calling me out again, out from the city of glass, steel, art, sound, Summer about to give way to Fall. Silence.

CHAPTER 8

Fifteen or so Women

A communion of saints began the day after our Mother died with women gathering at her house chanting Hail Mary. I arrived there on Sunday August 10 five days after she had died. The praying women would meet again on Tuesday and Wednesday night. They chanted, prayed for the soul of their dearly beloved Daisy. In the process they prayed for Tonika, one of our Mother's great grand-children who simply jumped around the hall. Hail Mary, Mother of God. The woman who led the prayers called; the others responded. There was no possession no talking in tongues, just a straight consistent repetition with emphasis placed on different sections of the chant each time it was repeated. Breathing changed. Mantras rose. Incantation, songs filled the house until the smell of brewed coffee crossed the living-room. Each of the two nights when I witnessed this communion of saints, they chanted for the soul of "our dearly beloved Daisy." It was happening on Earth where Daisy Augusta Andrew from the day she could speak her first prayer, believed in the forgiveness of sins, the resurrection of the dead and the life of the world to come. The communion of women used a Roman Catholic medium but that did not matter at least not to my Mother who, though Catholic, communed at any church as long as the Word of God was being preached. She was a fervent and faithful Caribbean Catholic.

At times the activity seemed useless to me. How did their prayers assure anything? What difference did their prayers make to her laying in a funeral home on ice? That was the logical me, the hurting me. Just as silence Revealed her mystery, so prayers called to a higher place not visible, not ends-driven, an act of faith, a communicative place beyond flesh, over any, above speech as spoken word. It is visible yet invisible like her fingers pressing thickly-loaded codes into mine.

This communion of saints, these fifteen or so women, forced reflection upon me. These women were doing something for their beloved sister. They were praying for her departed soul, one that lived among them. They were praying for its safe return. Throughout those nights, not more than two other men were present. I got the distinct impression that they were there because they knew and respected her in life, but really they came for drinks which accompanied such a gathering. My God, the emptiness I felt during those prayer sessions. I did not repeat the Hail Mary with the women, but took to muttering Psalms, her favourite Psalms. When I was whispering nothing, I simply looked on helpless. But those women? They were deep in a quality of confidence, a sort of assurance that transformed their very aura. The living room was electrified. The space felt like it was lit by candlelight, a softer, mystical atmosphere. Mama was being rewarded -- her sister-worshippers serving as mediums. I consoled myself within the lessons in silence, the moment, the warm unity among those prayer-women warriors, their prayer of confidence. She was loved and respected. It was well-known, and my sister Joycelyn reminded me over and over -- Mama helped so many people, Mama fed the community's hungry ones and had a word of encouragement to speak to those who were having a hard time even when her situation was worse. Help the weak if you're strong. Yet, my sister remembered that when she needed help, or just someone to caretake other than we her children, few cared to show up. Visits dried up over time. One-time friends passed outside her house, but no longer cared to call or come in. Those who utter Hail Mary now are her friends, the remaining few.

In the midst of this communion of saints, I thought about children who abandoned their parents, those who hated them. They must be bitter after they're gone. There are those who do not even taste bitterness. They do not share the weight of mourning. Little do they know that Love has its chemistry and just by observing a good deed one can experience an internal transformation. I was blessed by the actions of these women saints. Standing there among them, I asked what would it have cost those who disregarded their Mother in life. What was it that he or she was asking that was so difficult. In the blessed aura of rising prayers, I considered a universal sadness: in the development of human civilizations and communities we see the wonder and beauty of another only after they're dead. If only we could spring from this beauty and truth. If only these were the common platforms. In the case of a lost lover we may have the chance to say it: people can remain friends and say the sweetest things to each other after the relationship is over and each has found another. In the case of a dead lover it is nearly impossible. Dreams and visions may console but nothing beats presence, the actual form here laughing holding touching kissing sleeping running with or just being silent. There is great power in the real. When such power is blessed with the spirit of the living God the strength of Christ anoints, courses through that flesh and blood -- death is already defeated, swallowed up in victory, as Mama would say. Life is lived as if it were for eternity. We need feel the strengthening: we must know it not just believe it. Bob Marley. Listen to "Ride, Natty Ride." The matter remains, quickening flesh and blood, deepening know-how. Christ is not death. Spirit of Love communicates to the very core of soul, to tendons, ligaments and joints and sinews marrow cells genes, protein, microbiome and all that is yet to be discovered. In the history of Caribbean slave and liberation society Christ's gift is alive and active, as warming as yoga and the chant of Allah indeed, as blissful and quiet as the roll of sutras. Ooops. Did I offend? Bob Marley went as far as to say "Almighty God is a living man!" A living woman is supposed to be a strong woman an inspired woman. Christ resurrected is supposed to be eradication of misery and poverty hunger and disease in the life of this woman. Unreal, isn't it?

The body of a woman and man becoming a vessel full of energy? How could a man who died more than two thousand years ago be living in, energizing our hearts now? What does this tell us about structure and communicative capacity in hearts? What of Spirit's communication speed? And, are we to assume then that there has been a weakening of what was once a formidable yet mortal body? It is written that he took upon himself our sins, became like us to save us two thousand years ago. One thousand five hundred years later, Columbus sailed into the new world and slaughtered its people. Sins? Those Arawak and Kalinago peoples? They were glistening, at the very least, in harmony with nature. It is what we long for today, what we long to relate to. Is that not so?

CHAPTER 9

Interconnected Prayers, Interconnected Deeds

Few existing modern cultures openly practice communion with nature, not to mention elders and ancestral spirits. America's Founding Fathers are ancestral spirits, yet they would not be referred to as such. Kings and Queens of Europe are just the same. Those mid-nineteenth century fighters in the Caribbean left a magnificent legacy of struggle right up to the Workers Movement. The sayings of Simon Bolivar and Che Guevara are highly respected guidelines in Latin American society. The Sioux Indians produced a Chief named Seattle. The indigenous peoples of North America have been consistent about their ancestral territory, the sacredness of their burial grounds.

Think of this respect for ancestors with respect to Russia, China, India, Australia, Africa? Lots of people when you take to naming all Earth's countries, isn't it? Lots of communion of saints. Lots of remembrances, electromagnetic vibes. A communion of saints?

A woman falls from the deck of a fishing vessel in the Gulf of Mexico and swims twenty-seven miles to an oil-rig where she spray-paints SOS and is later lifted by helicopter. She movingly confessed praying to her grandmother to help her and save her from drowning. Her grandmother had died a few months before. She is Latina and Catholic. Indigenous beliefs and a Roman Catholic religious sensibility intertwined in a tensed struggle in a moment of real danger eliciting her veritably sacred practices. She connected with the person trusted most in life. Even if her grandmother was departed from the world of Water in which she struggled, she represented for her that beacon that voice which in life repeated: you can do it. In the cold of the moment there was no safer place to find warmth. There might well be a hierarchy of communion of Latina saints through which her grandmother herself whispered a word or made plaintive supplications -- an event which was instantaneous. It is very unlikely that English-speaking Caribbean Catholics would mention calling on their grandmother, though I am informed by my priest-friend that they're likely to call on saints; those who have done great human deeds and have passed on.

Yes, I've taken the freedom to invest my wake celebrants with a purity in action suggesting the gathering up of prayers and thanksgiving, suggesting the work of saints. They're not dead. Their intent is pure of heart. I am sure they would've called on Christ Jesus and God. They should then feel the swim, their muscles ready, their heart made brave, their hope of survival spoken by a soft voice, clear in its assurance: swim to the rig. You can make it! Indeed, while it is unlikely that the Dominican woman would call on their grandmothers for spiritual strength in an emergency, they're likely to believe that their grandmothers prayers delivered over their lifetime, would've guided them to safety. They'll tell you too that their Mothers and Grandmothers economic practices informed their everyday lives -- it will be to the region's socio-economic advantage when the same ancestral claim is made on the koud'main or the metayage as internal economic communion models. Communion? We behave sometimes as if we anticipate obliteration. Let us be clear. Hegemony still means control on all fronts. But something has been learnt lately about living community action. You can't take away a patois, a KwÉyòl, a sign a jazz step a lyric that does not wander aimlessly. Some internetted practices like the meetings of Dominican saints, or the business of pooling economic support, rooted, defined women's very existence, at least in my Mother's time. If we claim that a community sharing and helping spirit inherent in koud'main and metayage is dead, then we intuit their return in another shape or form albeit in part in our image and thus to be claimed as property and advanced, as basis for design in corporate team modules, single markets. Sharing hands? A coup de main? It's amazing what essence does. A simple cooperative practice initiated by women, sustained their community. Thing is, their sharing of food and pooling of money, the mutual care extended to each other's children kept the doctor away, kept the law at bay. They belonged to each other's religious communities, pushing the matter to glorious places -- they practiced being each other's keeper.

I say, Marx, Lenin, Trotsky, Sparrow, St. Paul and Mao informed C L R James as much as they did Walter Rodney and Maurice Bishop. Keynes informed Sir Arthur Lewis as much as Walcott chewed Shakespeare. Walcott could not have overcome without the Greeks, Lamming Brathwaite or Naipaul. This cross-pollination, this sharing of hands, ideas, is not simply colorful, but extends its breath into dance music theater painting art sculpture play-writing cricket even funeral wakes. True revolution and synthesis begins with a return when for example one recalls Sir Garfield Sobers and witnesses Brian Lara in full form. When another Vivian Richards goes to bat with another apartheid on his mind blazing at twenty-one years -- the mystic is blowing beyond the boundary. When David Rudder praises Slinger Francisco, when another Rudder is five and growing, the mystic is blowing. When another Chubby Mark, another midnight groover emerges in sixteen-year-olds in Dominica's music-scape, then we would not have worked in vain. When another Bob Marley unfolds in a Dominican, then truly, Justice plays an ancient hand.

You want to take the chance leaping with me for the first time, not having seen it, but believing that in spite of our troubles and issues in Christ, as Mama would say, all things are possible? Strange, how this sounds like seasons, cycles. Somebody goes, somebody comes. Someone dies, someone is born. One nation or race falls, another rises. Still within the domain of cycles and dharma, my thoughts were cast, even more so in New York with its non-stop vibrations. Tell you, its difficult standing in a New York house, receiving news of your Mother's death with an ocean between you two. Though this geography is nothing to Spirit and Thought, I contend that the real is real. It is good to see, hear, smell, touch even taste a beautiful form of flesh and blood within which the Spirit cared to sojourn. I had been with a Mother-Spirit for many years, and wished I were there when it was leaving her form. She instructs me that it does not matter. I continue weepingly.

CHAPTER 10

Mama's House

The afternoon I arrived from New York I went straight to my Mother's room. Her burial dress was laid out on the bed which I had bought her a few years past. She accepted the gift and like most Mothers asked about the price. It took me some time convincing her that the price of the bed did not matter. For an instant I saw her dressed in the two-piece peach laced at the bosom. I understood from my sister Joycelyn that she loved peach.

I decided to sleep in her bed that night, yet did not want to move the suit. How death changes perceptions! When night descended and it was time to sleep I walked boldly if not humbly into the room, lifted the pieces, placing them on a side but still together still not wanting to disturb their upper and lower placement. I did not sleep with my head at the bedhead, but across, giving the suit its space. It was as if she was in it but not in the flesh. I could not sleep. I smelled her, was frightened by the silence and a sort of authority demanding that I give it attention as it came through my body. She is my Mother, having had authority over my flesh and emotions at one point in time -- even at forty-seven I could not set aside its final execution. I longed to dream whenever sleep came to find her somewhere saying something. There was more to be revealed. Great events begin in silence.

Night two presented another unmovable, unflinching silence. I began to wonder whether I should go to my sister's house in order to find some rest. The dead was not the problem. My presence in the room did not disturb her over time and space in any way. My living consciousness could not immediately absorb the loss or the mystery of communication outside the visible or material world. I remembered both my Father and Mother saying to me the ability or capacity to do anything, is in you. The dead and death were not the problem. I realized mystery in absence though present. I was humbled. This was not a problem to be solved. Though I thought problem, this one was not in that category. Her absence held my attention, but I could not hold it, question it, look into its eyes; it was not visible. I don't know when I took to sleeping between absences and presences, but you know sleep, the way it operates; you only know you were in it when it's over, gone like darkness, Wind, Stars and Moon phases.

By night three part of the sleeplessness had been solved: the family had visited the funeral home and I had seen and touched her body. The last time I saw her she was silent. Now she is frozen inside. I always liked touching my Mother. Her hair was so beautifully silver. When she spoke I understood her brief remarks to be salient. And when she touched me this was a purity that a Father or another woman could never impart. That was the same hand that touched with tenderness and love and best wishes throughout my life. Yes, there was something salient in our communication. Of her eight children I was the one to have her dreaded eye disorder called glaucoma the sneak thief. We shared a visual connectivity! It is by way of our eyes that we will construct this return. I will not be alone in this adventure.

CHAPTER 11

The Crew

When our Mother died at eighty-one, six of her eight children were alive: Ketturah lived in London, Joycelyn in Dominica, Steinberg in New York, Pearl in Antigua, Ernest in Dominica and Albert in Miami. Pearl was particularly affected. She worked then, mainly as a midwife, and theater nurse at Holberton Hospital in Antigua. She visited Mama as often as she could -- sometimes rushing home on weekends when there was a sudden change in her condition. Albert was the last and as all lasts shared a special closeness to his Mother. He called frequently -- he was the one who informed me of her death.

Ernest had been at her side lifting her, taking her for drives when possible and bearing with her stubbornness when it arose. He visited each day before going to work.

Joycelyn was caretaker whose patience was stretched to bursting. Yet, she held on. She often told me "you never saw Mama when she was behaving bad." Joycelyn is the fourth child and the one who was responsible for the management of last rites.

Ketturah, Mama's eldest at sixty-five or six, did not make it home for the funeral. She had been away from Mama for so long I don't think she could relate anymore. If she could not bring herself to visit more than once in life, it was not in death when there was no living voice hand or eye that she could touch. I felt for her, my biggest sister: it must be hard for a first child not to be able to attend her Mother's funeral especially when they were both adults. She, however, made substantial financial contribution to cover funeral costs. I imagined my sister in her London apartment on her knees. The woman I had met in London in 1987 wept. She felt the hand: I wish I were there Dais to hold your hand as you took the last breath to thank you for carrying me in your womb at sixteen in a 1930s Caribbean.

It is a wonderfully-dressed phonetic compilation: my sister called her Mother Dais. In fact both of our Mother's first children called her Dais. The remaining six called her Ma and referred to her as Mama.

When our brother -- Mama's second child and first son – died at sixty-one in a London hospital I called Ketturah to allow Mama to speak with her. She cried like a baby blaming herself for not having looked more closely over her younger brother, at sixty-one. I remember telling my sister that I was about to put Mama on the line and she burst into crying telling me it was not her fault and the hospital was not prompt in its care. She anticipated having to give a report to Mother about her younger brother. In spite of her age she broke down as Mama was about to speak with her. It is as clear today in my mind. A Mother can have a serious impact on her child irrespective of the child's age. My eyes were opened to a world made complex.

CHAPTER 12

Weeping Back to New York

I left Dominica ten days after her burial knowing quite clearly that the next time I return to our house she would not be there sitting upright in silence or full of laughter. The house would be clean and still. Martina her last caretaker would not be there. How times change.

On my way back to New York I served as guide to an older man who was the Father of a friend living in the village where my family and I had lived for ten years before travelling to the United States. We shared drinks in Puerto Rico yet had to sit apart on American. We laughed again at JFK when our suitcases popped up at the carousel one after the other. My wife and her brother were there to meet me. She wore a red top and for a moment kept her distance before hugging me. The day of our Mother's funeral she called from New York and wept wishing she were there to help in the preparations. She was like a daughter to my Mother and whenever we visited she would go to her room and fall asleep next to her. We walked the balmy night and entered the vehicle. This is New York Mama, a place you never saw, a place you never will. This is going to be home for a while. Its glass steel and concrete structures stun imagination -- its labyrinths numerous, mind-boggling. I wanted to tell you about the train network which fascinated me from the first day I saw and traveled on it. I wanted to describe what I called the spirit of Manhattan in one of my poems. This is a complex social formation where your counsel on silence is so correct. I reported to my wife and your grandchildren. When I said as much as I could recall I headed for morning.

Temperatures left the eighties to hover in the seventies. It was going to be for me an autumn of the matriarch -- my preoccupation with wind and millions of leaves blown collectively along dim-lit streets under rain will not disappear easily I thought. They will rot and smell damp, conjuring forest spirits, wild-life force, wood-cutters, dreams and designs. Thoughts burst in novel places as if waiting for that fresh experience to open their eyes.

Between Dominica and New York Mama between your resting place and where I am, is an ocean itself rattling bones reparation rhythms your daughters remains in salt and algae, shelves rocks. Sunken master helmsmen notes, broken wheels, sharks dolphins whales, healing elements, coral calcium, the slime in conch, Haitian bones, sponges, half of sails, rudders skills, decks shafts wheelhouses treasures, what we called bullion at high-school, Kalinago pots, rigs, compasses. There is fire too in salt. You grieved as she crossed frontiers of oceans caught in currents between the Caribbean Sea and the Atlantic. It rings prophetic now, knowing that your third child's father was a ship's captain and her husband the same. Your faith was thrown to fragments in the unfathomable where losses are not reported since the sea does not speak to reveal the depth of its appetite for life with logic and regret. Eudora slipped into the dark high waters and you could not follow. There was no water-map neither did the rudder leave a trail. You wanted her body as most of those thrown up swollen but she never came back. This changed you forever. She is mingled now just as you are being mingled. Like you she returns in the clouds and rain suspended in Sun's fire. A body lost at sea is not merely lost. Ripped from its sure gravity, it is subject to a savage surgical procedure -- lungs erupting bleeding and unconsciousness. Your faith was challenged. You could not administer last rites, touch, dress her dark thick anatomy. You hoped she had a chance in all her fear to whisper a prayer. Grief kills.

Bernard, your first son, that is, your second child died in a London hospital. He was buried in England. Where are the bodies? The ocean and city on the river have taken the bodies away, Mama. You once asked me what was it I was thinking in this small head of mine. In this New York, I am thinking of you Mama. I am thinking of thousands and thousands of other women, their backs pressed against the ground in exchange for a few dollars. I see millions of women of your color jammed into cotton cane and tobacco fields criminalized with no medical care no justice. I see your white linens, red, your head-ties disheveled your sanctity ruptured, defiled. I think of thousands of nights and mornings on your knees wailing the Lord is your shepherd -- you were not supposed to want. I heard you say he restoreth my soul. I still believe that your soul was not the matter. It was your want.

I still struggle with my ways -- remembering you handing me the Bible to read that section from Psalm 119 counselling "how shall a young man cleanse his ways? By taking heed according to your word." Recognizing the cleansing power, the young man responded thankfully "with my whole heart will I seek you. Do not let me wander from your commandments." The discipline, the love is incomparable. Her Christ-teachings, say what you need about them, opened the eyes of my heart later in my adult life. Yet, I was helpless as her sight sneaked away.

Joycelyn reminded me that on many occasions after work Mama would visit friends and relatives and on her way home would fall on tree roots in the dark. Her knees were bruised she said. How could someone so lovingly discerning and insightful be deprived of her ability to see those she loved fed and nurtured? Troubles me, and it should, considering her faith. Faith should work right down to the cell's membrane, shouldn't it? It seems however, that when we use the hand we lose the hand. The part used to make a living is the part that fails. I have heard this many times. Why. Indeed this is no longer a question to be asked regarding the life and times of Daisy Augusta Andrew. It is an international question. In the present scheme of things it may even be considered rhetorical.

I saw a television documentary about a man who was an accomplished architect, having designed New York's most magnificent structures, and paradoxically he fell just outside a toilet at Penn Station New York and died there. Strange opposites, isn't it? There is another story of a woman who became an oncologist saving the lives of many women until she spotted a lump in her breast, in her body. Fortunately she beat it and became a better oncologist. Is the gift hidden in the curse? At what stage in human development did life become so seemingly permanently dual? To every act of decomposition there is a concomitant act of recomposition and composition in the living. Primitive tissue knows primeval vegetation. Those constituting cells in the heart know the hawk's cry, expansion of pines rings, the ancient course of the Milky Way. Chief Seattle reminded those who came to deforest: the sap of the tree is the blood of my brother. His brother is also a tree. To cut down one is to take away his brother's life-blood. The heart carries blood in motion warm, producing heat rooted in Fire, itself a transporter of life -- oxygen in the boukan's blaze the volcano's awakening, the baby's first cry. Seasons of the heart are in phases of the moon its rise and fall its dark absences and eclipses its romance with tides and smiles of a fetus. Island influences? Were that media announced the birth of every child under the Sun, Moon and Stars! Who knows, there may well be deep underlying correlative structures between death and happiness birth and sadness globally -- a way of seeing, shifting now to a celebration of Life! In new York reflection is becoming effervescent.

Tell you, the island in which this woman is buried is just under three hundred square miles. Its highest mountain reaches 4747 feet. One has to be lucky to see Morne Diablotin its highest, from the town of Portsmouth. Most times it is covered in mist almost as if commanded by its elfin vegetation to do so. I love the local name of one of its rain forest trees: the Châtaignier. The islands 3500 Kalinago peoples called it Waitukubuli. Somehow I remember that meant land of many battles. Today it means tall is her body. Its national anthem sings of an "isle of beauty / isle of splendor." A Trinidadian once said that if there was any music in heaven it had to be pan. If heaven had a favorite color, the Dominican replied, it had to be green, many thousands of shades of green. Soil there is rich. The island's gray west-coast and southern soil its black-sand beaches bubbling fumaroles and sulphur springs, clearly mark volcanic origin. Its flora exudes thousands of healing qualities feeding its soil as much with billions and billions of their fallen nutrients and when rain comes they too slip under another strata. They too give life to life. They have no blood nor language yet their death sustains, assures a shape and form like and unlike themselves. The manicou and agouti eat of their substance and the boa slides beneath, across their surfaces along heavy tree trunks, branches holding nests and fruits, with nuts and coated seeds on their edges. Dominica's three hundred and more rivers network paths with stunning flexibility bending to floods, seasons, moons and the call of the seas. A caterpillar still becomes a butterfly there. Birds may fly all the way from North and South America investing their melodies in seasons. Rivers rush from a southern valley bearing healing sulphur minerals East. It is an ecologist's paradise -- a tall holistic landmass where battles have raged for centuries between those who realized significance in its geographic location its archipelagic centrality. There is a secret too to this tumultuous green purply mass to be found not only in stars circumnavigating its northern space, charting each birth and death hurricane and rebellion. Those who shout esoteric shall someday claim their natural property, their birthright.

People live long there. In fact death and birth are constantly in love in nature there. In the island's northern town of Portsmouth, some two hundred yards to the west of the Roman Catholic cemetery is the quiet chop of the Caribbean Sea. A few yards to the south of the Catholic cemetery stands an Anglican church and in its yard its cemetery. I remember as a child, people were scared to walk the road between the Anglican church and the Roman Catholic cemetery, except those living in the area who never exhibited any fear walking through the Catholic cemetery itself. Two cemeteries side by side? How ingenious the orthodox. How intriguing is midnight here! How beautiful a third hour when sleep slips to descending even on the watchman.

But now under sunlight descending in the West, I stood with others watching the coffin lowered, listening to the strings of Leonel's guitar as the choir did its final bidding. My daughter Roberta was next to me having come all the way from Houston to pay her last respects to a woman she loved. I asked her a futile question: is there another way of putting away the dead? Not that I did not know the body could be burnt. It was one of those rhetorical moments spawned by helplessness. She did not read futility. She whispered that in Houston there are cases in which thieves come to the grave-site after the burial, dig up the soil take the body out of the coffin and sell the varnished tree. It must be shocking, grievous for relatives when they discover the unearthed body of their loved ones. This event unsettled intelligence.

The soil around the grave-side was brown and wet. Those few men who agreed to cover the body cared little about clothes and shoes. One friend of many years, Augustus Williams, told me he was doing this for Miss Daisy, as he picked up a spade. I simply stood, looking on as the soil grew higher. Yes, I stood as the cemetery emptied, as those who followed her moved on to their homes and communities. I was going to be alone even in the crowd. I could feel the emotion announcing itself, cruelly informing me of its coming. When all had gone, I sat with my friend, Augustus Williams, looking over the decorated site. He respected my silence. I was not sad, neither was I joyful. I was somewhere sinking without fear.

Later in my emptiness as evening relinquished its last strains of light, I looked out at the Caribbean Sea from the flat concrete roof of my sister's house searching naively for signs of a departing spirit. Only its silence reminded me of silence and that existed long before she was born. On the flat Caribbean Sea surface, like glass now in semi-darkness, I wished for a wavelet, a simple curve, a sea-gull something that shattered or tickled the silence and the Sea did not seem to know my desire. In seeking her wave, I could come upon others -- so many hands lifting and falling, floating, sinking. I thought that by singing one of her favorite songs I would be relieved of the emptiness but that only comingled in the Wind and Wind is never seen. Even if I was born in the midst of a hurricane I did not learn to talk with or to

Wind. Still amazes me how Christ Jesus did it from a state of rest! Then I began to wander, searching a thought, deliberately calling a memory akin to ocean life. Maybe this would connect. Imaginably, I might see something that was not there, but think it was there anyway. I began to feel happier that she had sent me out to see at a very early age vomiting my inside out cleansing the body protecting my youth from the wrath of evil spirits. At least that was the folk wisdom: no evil could affect those who crossed the ocean. I was a huckster then until I experienced the fury of Martinique's southern channel. I told her I did not want to go back. She sent me up north to St. Kitt's to sell the final batch of plantains, tannias and oranges anyway. I had to pay my high school fees and buy the texts. It could be that the sea was telling me something on that flat roof that day when she was buried but I could not immediately understand sea language. The sea was saying, relaying something to me, but I was not listening, I was not looking at it as it was, but as I wanted it to be. Sea texts? Except for the fisherman the sailor the surfer the oceanographer and lighthouse watchman I know few people who read such books. They are as cryptic as scrolls from the Dead Sea or waters holding African spirits in their dark bellies and the connectivity of the collective unconscious. Here a shell does not celebrate difference, neither does a coral reef say to the teeth I know you not. Here a camel passes through the eye of a needle and a child sits in the hurricane's wind in remains of a crumbled house. It is here that dead fauna feeds flora and buried bodies nourish tree roots. Here green sparkles in a leaf and mimics laughter of a country child river-bathing under a midday sun. Here a hand that gives receives even when that which is received is not visible, tangible. Job in his book, was truly silent when asked whether he knew where morning begins. Observe. mourning becomes dancing and dying becomes birthing. Indeed in living the dancer becomes the dance. A thought longs to fly South in Winter and Spring to tango with Summer. Summer? I could not welcome joy rising. It was unnatural to the mourning mind and heart. Joy? Not joy at this moment as I looked out to ocean, the port's double-breasted Cabrits, two lovely chunks of round mountain, forming the nose of this handsome, pretty, rugged island, dangerous to love, dangerous to hate. Summer? Mothers in our time knew Summer's gifts, its freedoms, its triggering indiscipline, its waywardness. I'm traveling again, traveling on the beatless beat of this ocean stretching far West without a sunken Sun, far placid wonder. Summer? From that roof I visualized us on water, basking in longevity island's Summer, consuming papaya guavas bananas oranges grapefruits plums mangoes nuts soursop cashew kashima cherries tangerines sucking fatpoke tamarind kennips, tearing cane. We bathed and bathed till whitened by salt. While a few people on island went to the sea to have a soak children said they bathed. Rivers had deep sections in those days. We called them basèns. We would dive till we were cold. We eat so much of what grew around us, plus what our kitchens produced, not to mention what we ourselves concocted, that our Mothers would have to wash us out in preparation for school in September chanting prayers as she basked us in leaves ripped off branches from trees growing in our yard plus what she gathered from dada or the yard of another woman. It must have been during the new moon or the crescent's passionate love for its neighboring star. We take what's around us and under our skin for granted. They're connected. It was a connection you knew Mama. It was a connection Mothers in our yard knew; Mothers in our land, our community knew from their Mothers who came to know from their Mothers. Cleansing, purging, colonics. This was also protection dating to the earlier days of medicine when superstition reigned. Yes there is the dark side. It was far from my childhood and adolescent thoughts, but it was there in our charming island, mingled with Mama's cleansing and our innocence. Perhaps too, the belief that people are all good is couched in my early education and socialization, overwhelming this dark that even as an adult, I refused to look at though it surfaces in and around me.

I started having a sense of a dark side when our Mother began losing her mobility as her sight diminished. I had not thought of a dark side before. It meant to me the hidden an uncovered. It could be enshrined in an unexpected life experience, the behavior of a relative or friend or just a mode of what I considered unfair initially. Essentially, some things did not connect. In my thinking there is beauty in light as much as in darkness. By darkness I do not mean evil touching the biblical sons of men preferring darkness to light. How would King Solomon have praised God's handiwork? The Magi saw a star. Actually, St. Lucia's Literature Nobel-Laureate Derek Walcott wrote to a green night. I thought it surrealist. Then, I saw a full moon on a green island. Out of the forms distrusted may come the most brilliant. Poetry's green night? Darkness has shown so much of nature's beauty in our part of the world that it is not possible to speak of it naively as evil, a place of hiding for the wicked, or a medium for carrying out lawless acts. The military loves it. Lovers need to reclaim dark nature's trust, its keeping of hearts secrets, vows made in honest, words spoken in truth and beauty against a tree trunk bending to night's light groove. Darkness? Trinidad and Tobago's David Rudder sang that out of a "muddy pond" ten thousand flowers will bloom. In spite of this aesthetic flight, I became increasingly aware that evil had become sophisticated, but remained evil. Our people knew its crude, indigenous peaks -- soucouyants, diables, people turning into animals, women flying on broomsticks decorated as if in a majestic act, men raising dead bodies to ask of their knowledge and power. The dark Caribbean side, power and knowledge? Who were they mimicking, these men and women with Africa under their skin, Europe breathing its hellish economic language like a blaring carnival band? They drew from all, I tell you, making geographic adventures, adventures not restricted by prescribed rules of early ritualist representation. They flew before yogis came with levitation. I call this religious experimentation. There were women who arrived at doors of Roman churches first to knock at it; those who took the communion symbol into their bosom; those who jumped over wash-basins; those in transition between nun and African seer, healer. What were they in search of, terrifying families, horrifying children, isolating themselves in community, central in the church yet dwelling on the brink of a mischievous interpretation. Sometimes I felt like loving their mystery, its magic, its seeming power and secrecy. They looked like people who evolved from trees in community standing and unknown. My hometown community? I needed to walk off this flat roof, down the stairs to a social setting, to those gathered, to those leaving for my Mother's house. I needed to reflect on something saner like sports, music she loved, hymns she sang, ice she crushed with her hard teeth after lunch as she walked out for the idling jeep to take her to work. This was better, lighter, relevant to mourning, memory's respected production. Maybe, it was better to think about glaucoma, medicine, sight. But this took me back to a quality of darkness. Did not matter. Whatever came to thought came to thought to be thought. And even as thoughts tilted their wings in darkness now and electricity, I could not help noticing how time had slipped by, how my Mother was covered. Like all of us, she was to be reduced to bone and dust, ash and sometimes nothing, always nothing, still something. Had to be something. Has to be something. I'm weeping now!

CHAPTER 13

The Gene Thing and Profound Perception

To have been born in a world where darkness is evil and light is good and to experience a gradual shifting into darkness through sight loss, anxiously double-beats the heart, sufficient to trigger an emotional imbalance. There were no medical answers no solutions except those in bottles. Most ophthalmologists then and now had never been blind and back. Think of how many blind and visually impaired prayed for the answer: receive your sight. One also has to understand a Caribbean/ Dominican society in transition or crisis -- a movement from herbal medicines to an adoption of medical science and positioning of the pharmacy.

In Dominica, at the dawn of the 80s a surgeon provided optometric services. Visual impairment medication then was Pilocarpine, Timolol and Diamox in tablet form. By the late eighties into the nineties we witnessed the arrival of Alphagan, Cusopt and Xalatan. Diabetes would be more directly connected to visual impairment in public health by the mid to late eighties, and surgery became a clearer choice by 2000.

I don't remember my Mother mentioning consistent use of any herbs seeds or dietary patterns in eye care, though there must have been plants at the very least among the Kalinago. She depended wholly on the medical profession and yet this was a woman who knew every other herb in which her children should be bathed. She was not alone. My Mother trusted eye doctors. And why shouldn't she? 70s practitioners in Dominica were creditable diagnosticians who succeeded in obliterating many illnesses. Granted, patients seldom asked questions. The doctor was like the priest and the lawyer. Remember too that on islands, the four respected professions coming out of the 50s, 60s and 70s were law, theology, engineering and medicine. In many ways too, doctors were personal and patients followed meticulously the regime prescribed by them. Poor people's children were not prominent in the field until the 80s, and when they would appear, the profession had taken on the business mien and attitude. By the mid-90s, forty patients at the doctor's office did not receive much individual attention even though they believed the profession had improved technologically. The closest she came to local or herbal treatment was through her grandson, Ketturah's first child. In the late seventies, he had been living in London for a while and was a student of histology. He was also Rastafarian and brought her a package of herbs which she was supposed to draw. I recall she reporting that that was doing her well until death struck. Unfortunately -- and this may well be a reflection from the dark side -- Teddy died in a traffic accident on September 23, 1985. He was twenty-seven. She mourned his violent passing, untimely as it seemed. Whatever connection cord she held with London by way of Ketturah was being ruptured. At the beginning of the 90s when she could walk around with assistance, efforts were being made to get her to visit Bernard her first son, and Ketturah, Teddy's Mother, both resident in London. In an interview with the British Consular Office representative, she intimated that she was blind. She was not granted the visa. She said I told them the truth.

This whole issue of blindness began feeling like a had to happen, a phenomenon to which an explanation was available medically but as for a cure that remained elusive both to patient and doctor. My search began when my Mother told me after a long conversation on the matter: "please forget about the gene thing," the runs in families medical school discourse. In fact the literature consolidated an unimpeachable triangulation among diabetes, high blood pressure and visual impairment. Physicians and ophthalmologists I met, said they ran for decades in families and nothing could stop them running. A culture of helplessness was being constituted; a subtle dependency code being drafted for the body. We were now victims of our family history even as that history was being vigorously negated. No matter what you did or became you were to be humbled by this arbiter operating not only in your daily negotiations and exchange practices but in your body self. There was no way to stop this, they reported. There was empirical evidence. Family members in whom the runs-in-the-family issue broke were in the great-grand and grand category, were dead or near dead with no historic explanation left, not even one of the flowers serving as salve to the eye when used as a wash, or the bitter one cleansing blood. Karma? Traces? They were being subsumed, revived and subsumed again.

In the mid to late 80s, media in Dominica, health officials and politicians were all espousing the "new" health paradigm: the individual is responsible for his or her health. People were suddenly being referred to as "persons." "Individuals," "consumers" and "clients" would follow in a sort of commodification of the self -- commodification, reification and fetishism not being subjects of interest in medical school, among students of medicine. The shift was dramatic in an island where historically the doctor/patient relationship was dominated by the former.

Foods changed. The market became free. By the dawn of the 90s, cysts and fibroids were increasingly common in women in their twenties. One gynecologist attributed this physiological change to dietary change; young women were not eating what their land produced. In fact, bits of the same food were placed on plates of those who were visually impaired. Salt, flour, sugar, oil, butter, little exercise -- the eighties took off this way. Thing is we had always used these, but those products either dropped in natural quality, and people became less physical and outdoor-oriented with arrival of cable television. Politically, it was a new time; new was everywhere in products, in taste. Consumption became the new medium. New was the word. But there were constants. Few cared about cause. You see, when -- and it's a big when -- ophthalmology ever comes to care about cause, its focus will shift from the eye alone. Significantly therefore, an ophthalmologist will have a nutritionist as partner in her/his office sharing evidence and income. Now, that may be difficult for ophthalmology's monolithic episteme. Nothing new. It might have been difficult for ophthalmology to accept scientifically, that as the hours of the day changed, intraocular pressure change. I was beginning to believe that ophthalmology has not struggled to cure, though I wanted to give its practitioners the benefit of the doubt. The formulae for producing a drug to more effectively deal with AIDs and cancer was being held behind glass ceilings. Politics of medicine? The eye? I cannot believe that those who care for the eye as profession, would not like to see others see. But I've observed their helplessness; their body language says the same.

In 2001 in Dominica an ophthalmologist told me most times during their training they watched people with glaucoma go blind and could do nothing about it. This visual disorder and its cure particularly, was not on their radar. Over the last 100 years, Cure has not been within their training domain either. Glaucoma they contended and propagated, runs in families. It is a gene thing and had to be left to its course, treated at the very least, but that was all. Truth is, sight loss management is lucrative business. Epistemologically, the eye as organ of study is still part of a whole known as the human body, indeed, an extension of the brain. To them however, the eye had no direct connection to the pineal and pituitary gland, hypothalamus the thyroid stomach liver, intestines or breathing apparatus. Understandably, interpretation of overwhelming glaucoma symptoms proved too much for our Mother at the time. Surely, it is still too heavy for many partials who simply take the medication trickling down their nasal passages along the lining of their throats, bitter. After a few years, partials don't complain about tingling side effects any longer -- they have to be so careful in their unfriendly environment. One thing is for sure: she was forever challenged. She did not tell, I did not ask and therefore did not know the daily terror she faced running into glass, pillars, opened doors, slipping on steps when descending, having no distant view, struggling with veils of fog, mist, dark, grey, hit by sunlight to blinding, truly blinding, rising each day to the same tightness in ciliary muscles, the same trouble, the same horror. Depression descended, frustration alighted, landed and would not take off. Thoughts were scattered, yet she focused to the final number, round, praying, hoping.

Not only did she develop excellent hearing skills; she began talking about events that did not obviously occur. First she complained that both her house and land were being taken away. She would call the names of those who were taking them. She would ask me Stein where are we. She would feel the walls. She would say that we are outside despite what I tell her, how I assured her that we were in her house. There was also the story of the police who had arrested one of our brothers whom she had seen and spoken with a few minutes before. Ernest, so cool, would smile but sometimes it sounded instructive to me. It was the call to be watchful. In her depressed state, she always had an appointment with a lawyer in the capital to rectify a property matter. She would mention these things with a certainty that anyone not knowing her condition would believe her. Maybe there was some truth to her symbolism, her power of discernment!

Look, on the day of her funeral I played usher. One of her eldest relatives came into the church assisted by our cousin Elma, since she used a walking stick. I followed the two to the far right of the church. The two central sitting areas were almost taken up. When this elder woman had been seated I sat with her and thanked her for summoning the courage to come. She replied that she would always come for Dais. She lifted the bottom of her dress revealing her strapped knee. I again thanked her and walked to the back right where I saw a woman seated. She was in the church but did not seem to be part of the funeral service. I approached this person engrossed in a small book. I said "good afternoon and thanks for coming to my Mother's funeral." She turned with what seemed to me at the time to be anger almost awakening from her self. I had disturbed her. She appeared to me as two in one, that is, to have two faces. I asked who are you and she told me her name in full. My meditation that day was too high to be terrorized. I shivered into depth awareness. It was the same name of the same family that my Mother for decades, for years, kept mentioning -- the same people who were taking away her land and house. Seemed that they kept keys to Earth and Heaven, Life and Death. Honest. I had not met this woman before. Never knew her. I only heard her name from my Mother. In this full church I walked straight to her. She corroborated. This lady was using the service as a medium. She was not the only one. It dawned on me that after all, our Mother must've been right about some property, some value being held captive, indeed, some evil practice. What made her right? There was no tangible evidence that her property was being taken. Could she have been so materialistic that even in her blindness and aging she craved control over things? How do we account for the fact that she was so specific in naming the individuals. Could she have been using a death metaphor to indicate her slow departure. Could she have been signaling the crash of that body, the crash of the gates, the gradual dissipation of sense of taste. Could she have been approaching the days described by King Solomon in Ecclesiastes when a rustling leaf disturbs, speech slurs and, limbs no longer have strength to carry the body and thus diminishing reason? Could such diminishing hold moments of discernment, transcendence? How could I have walked straight to this woman in a church full of hundreds? Yes. Mama was right on. She intercepted a community activity outside her personal state and loss. She interpreted loss. What remains instructive is that her utterances were Most times clearly true. Implicitly, they caused us to be watchful. And there were times when we dismissed them as absurd, not realizing that absurdity bears lessons to thinking, but thinking may not listen! How fortuitous it was that the spirit should have directed me to that critical connective tissue in that church! This woman was surprised. I had found her at last. I had intercepted her communication, albeit, one being conducted within ritual, inside dogma to perpetuate control, subjection of a family and people, a single Mother of eight and her children. Ah. It seemed to me that this woman was embedded in this lifetime project of suppression. What futility. Note. She was at the heart of the church, respected and well-known, perpetuating an evil as if there were no living Spirit moving in this God place. Justice, shouldn't our Mother have been angry? I looked at the woman and could've buried her with her guilt protruding!

CHAPTER 14

Underwater Image and the Gene Thing

In the early years of her restricted mobility our Mother was not angry. She somehow believed that she would see even up to her early seventies. But as the prospect grew less and her depression intensified she broke loose from her moorings. It seemed a time to rage. My sister Joycelyn and brother Ernest knew better than the rest of us how violently aggressive she could be. She was heavy, not physically fat, and when she decided not to move, her body descended into a coherent Buddhist solidity. When she dropped her weight within, force was not a wise option -- she grew more stubborn. She wore away the patience of the most patient and yet she was Mama. We could not abandon her. This is not only because she did not abandon us. Without speaking it she kept us bonded to her through her difficulties, her trials. We could have left her house frustrated on Thursday night but would wake on Friday to find her again maybe still dazed after little sleep and, quiet. I think she heard the dawning sound of each day. We simply had to adjust. She was in limbo. She appeared trapped between her physical and spiritual world and the latter was not penetrating to the former. The tradition said wait on the Lord, be courageous, and your heart shall be strengthened. This fine tradition, its vital force or Living Word did not electrify, balance body and mind to produce a cure in her? From her darkness she saw some light and maybe that was all she had to achieve in this phase of her life. Those who came after had to restructure and flood with light and fire.

On many occasions I remember questioning my rational mind. What if Mama was seeing something we could not understand. Why was it that what she said made sense to me. What if what she claimed so positively was yet another product another symptom of a tortured mind, the, a thickly-covered optic nerve. On reflection she too, was traveling the road of images. One could almost call it prophetic but with caution considering her visual field. She said she saw writings on the wall. It was literal. She reported actually seeing words being written or appearing. She would be upset when I did not confirm or agree that I saw the same. I truly did not see writings -- at least not what she was seeing on the wall, at least not yet. Was I with seeing eyes too blind to see? I could not see that other world, the one which presented itself to her so easily in the midday sun. In the midst of conversation she would see someone standing over me. She would ask me to speak softly. The man standing over me was so close and still she believed if we spoke softly enough the apparition would not hear. She cautioned me constantly: speak softly. A soft answer turns away, disappoints wrath, she instructed me. A soft answer absorbs, comprehends with quiet incision, seals the contents of wrath: it falls on all comes to all visits all. A soft answer is not easy to produce. Wrath is a sort of absolute Anger, a force that respects no one like a hurricane. Some people's choices are full of wrath by the very nature of choice made. A soft answer is out of rhythm with wrath's discord. A soft answer silences wrath, disturbs its intention. An action stirred in and by the spirit leads to discovery of the good and wicked.

Just when I became impatient with her images, her story, she would launch another. Just when the writing on the wall, the land-thieves episode, the man standing overhearing our conversation story became slightly irritating because I could not immediately see what she said she was seeing, she presented another film, another idea, I dare say… My Mother, in the height of her visual tightness, told me a fascinating story about an underwater system that controlled everyone on Earth by way of cameras. She said they could see everybody. I thought of omni vision and omniscience and even the capacity for circumnavigation. She asked whether there were cameras in her house because she was of the impression that we were being watched. Now this is Dominica. This is not a Fascist or Communist state. This is not a totalitarian condition. To grasp this one, I had to cross, transcend national frontiers. This was not the eye of a woman in the community "who" gossiped, or the tongue of an unemployed man in a small town. This one had to be installed, hooked up, panned and zoomed either by a person present, from a distance, possibly by an alien master control. This one caught my attention. I was adrift, too soon on the surface of a place I loved. In part, the Sea had been my childhood home, my vacation spot, my geography lesson. On too many occasions its surface was too blue, too dark blue, too beautifully strong. The Sea is so vast under! From beneath the ocean? Cameras looking at us? Cameras were looking at us while we looked at what they manufactured on prime time. You're right Mama. They were everywhere -- at street corners, at stop lights, in restaurants, hotels, supermarkets, theatres, banks, in our flatscreens wherever. This is the nature of information societies. But in your house? Under the Sea? Sub-stations to satellites to earth stations Mama? Somebody would have to install them and we did not own a dish.

She stared in the distance as if over a submarine plain, its shelf, its distant strip of teeming life, their multiple colors. A whale? Its whistle? What are you hearing, what are you seeing Mama? How is under the ocean captured, balanced, held in your head, a mere rock on the ocean's floor, a grain, a shark's broken tooth. Why doesn't the sea cleanse your eyes, burst through your hardened tears? Why don't the image's catalyze chemistry, crystallize into tissue? Thoughts. Are they not strong here, touching, being the force of nature itself? What is it Mama? What is it that you see, that holds your attention? Is it an image from yesterday's history lesson of death by water? Is this another lost book on slave homicide opening? Or are you seeing life abundant, birth-place of reefs, fish-life so rare? What is this mirroring your brain's energetic, effortless silence? There is something out there. There was something out there, but she did not appear threatened. Was this a result of a spiritual connect with her daughter? Cameras?

The all-seeing had entered or returned. It was in the world. It is in the inner world. Initially, it seemed an alien at the very least a human creation, a mere figment of her imagination, her tired thoughts, those given to effortless flight devoid of human intention and thus outside neuro-boxes, shot out of orbit finding renewed velocity. Along the path you observed men busy at work, not necessarily under the Sea. A wise tongue knows depth. It was a system of international surveillance. What seminal truth to the ears of a communication studies major! She whispered. She might have encountered the half-brother of an Orwellian image. She might have sojourned in spirit at that house of water having started her departure long before her brain said no, or her heart ceased and her breath danced into Heaven's orbit. It could be satellites, large populations in dense settlement patterns in which everybody looked into everybody else's life file. I hear hegemony. I hear the departure of privacy. It is dangerous when we cannot speak free. There appears to have been a rule in her days which stated that one should not speak a thought if one was not sure that what the thought describes exists. There was a quality of method in her madness. Repression, telecoms, surveillance, control over distance, fear of free expression, privacy invasion -- these form and represent part of the foundation on which modern civilizations legitimize their interests, coerce and force their citizenry. In fact, citizenry in their private world of dreams and visions see that world of control, but may as well attribute its appearances to divine intervention, depression, a dream, a vision or just another of night's regular occurrences. Seldom does it mean to them on interpretation, an expression of political force, save when its contents are collectively articulated. Truth is, the spirit does not know class differences when it seeks vessels for carriage and execution of justice. But, do those who come from the working class who carry in them manifestations of the prophetic, ever come to light? Are answers to the world's crisis already in the world, always were in the world, but do not surface, because those who realize its presence in their minds, hearts and souls do not own the means to transmission? Spirit should break down all walls. Or is it about to.

By way of women such as Daisy Augusta, it seems to me that spiritual engagement begins when individual capacity ends. Still amazes me that such faith did not burst through blockages in the trabecular meshwork during moments of anger and subsequent sleep. To me, she had the kind of faith to receive her sight. I gather she would prefer that I read this as God's will to be advanced.

Stein you must pray. Go to church. How is the eye. What's the time. She was trying to determine whether I could still see. Too many times I could not tell her that my vision was being blurred or I was losing it peripherally. I did not want her to be worried about me but she insisted on asking. She wanted truth irrespective. At the very least, she could whisper a prayer with direction. Telling her the truth would make her comfortable and set her thinking within its maternally intuitive domains. Experience had taught that the weight of the subject changes with time. Truth hurts damages even destroys. It finally releases. And I speak here about talking with a parent. When I would finally tell her the state of my eyes, she listened intently with her head bowed not sadly but in a mode that caught each word and directed each utterance to a place of answers. She obviously did not want me to express regret and lifted her head when in my half anger I noted that I did not ask for this. Small mind. I rambled for about fifteen minutes. She summarized the matter. She said, "please, forget about that gene thing." Silence! There was always a break, a pregnant pause as if to take in the history of the moment, the movement, to draw on their relevances, glasses of water, nuts, bits of fruit, examples, reasons, purpose. Forget? This was at the heart of modern reasons for disease. How could I forget about the gene thing. Silence. There was a larger matter coming beyond frontiers of the gene thing. My Mother was pushing me outside the field of scientific consensus, over against a dominant paradigm. But I am sure she did not intend for me to be in argument over the matter, but she came to this radical conclusion, presenting it to me for consideration, if not intellectual engagement. Speak softly. If you're going to consider this gene matter, practice. Vulgarity in intellectual matters? I might commit it, but she did not condone it. Language communication? Even in speech's grammar, I had to be careful. That was not unusual. We shared silences and a deep-talk relationship. She could talk on any matter using humor anecdote proverb or something she heard from radio to beef up conversation. With her I did not have to censor my language use, and speech, speaking had to be well conducted with grammar intact. It was and is a fine tradition. Speak the language correctly. Just imagine how significant this tradition was to my French-trained philosopher Father. I was truly torn between two lovers and feeling good. But she listened. She did not simply hear. I know many people who hear talk but do not listen to make conversation. This quality of communication allowed us to grow closer as we grew older. It is the pleasant nature of the woman that I loved, her willingness to make conversation, her knowledge and appreciation of good. It was her never-ending energy and calm in the midst of greatest difficulty. It was her sincerity, her openness, plus what she referred to as her sense of knowing her place. Surprise? I gather she gave me the final silence three months before she died. How could I ever doubt its benefits? Or, how, looking back on it now can I ever doubt the amazing capacity of Mothers to collect their children's lives, indeed, to find that single element depicting character at the center of their beings. Mothers observe No matter their class or education. Mother could spot behavior change in an instant. With that kind of insight, she avoided being judgmental. This could lead to faultfinding. That was not the nature of her person. Her observations, spoken gently and clearly, were intended to correct without offending.

In the days when it was not possible to see faces she would identify people by their voices and the touch of the hands. Whenever my children visited, she would touch them all over remarking how plump they were and how much they had grown. She would not eat until she was quite sure that everyone had food though everyone wanted her to be fed first. And isn't this Mother universally? From the very beginning, Mother's presence, Mother's person represented feeding, nurturing. From Earth, to its oceans and the human body, Mother symbolized an outpouring of sustenance from fruit to fish to milk, though today, the real food pouring from woman's breasts is used less and less in the protection of an infant from disease. Indeed, world powers today modify weather. Heia, temporary power keepers modify the world's food, its power of perceiving and reality construction. In truth, children themselves choose differently. Their foods are fast and all around them vibrantly sold by way of media. They are assailed by the same, believing them to be offering choices.

In our days, we used lots of fish; when a fowl was killed it was one from our yard. When beef was used, it was from cattle slaughtered the same day or the one before. Pig meat was salted, smoked over the smoke from rising fire for preservation. How food has changed!

While our Mother was rushing out of the house to meet an idling vehicle sent to take her to work at Geest Industries she would shout, "all you share." "All you" is very English Creole and may be read as you all must share though this does not quite capture the bloodline. Two ideas are encapsulated here: the eldest should do the sharing and we should not be angry over what we receive -- essentially, let there be equality.

In those days we eat food. It was food nurtured, cultured in soil giving life to all receiving it all, seeds dying before breaking in and to water and warmth before unfolding and gently surfacing in a quality of air charged by nuclear. We grew out of the nourishment of our own. We did not name it or call it organic. We knew no other. The little field so many cultured kept us away from the doctor.

Mama your world of endless cameras sees and records what the majority eat. Camera owners supply. The customer who is always right keeps coming back for plus. The old conditioning technique is modernized: it is more openly and sensually conducted. Truly I don't know when and where large took off but size is in with the modification of the gene thing. You do not have to ask for it. It is taken for granted that you eat excess and leave. This is the merit of the meal. In principle, the medical profession sounds the alarm alerting the pharmaceutical industry that an army of obese forms is just about to climb the hill over the valley, if it can climb. Vulgar? When climbing is difficult, there is something for energy, for overcoming the mount to the valley of desserts. Consequently, many children in these big cities are dragging not only their pants but the weight of their bodies. It is true: only the living can harm the living to death. It is also true that dead food kills. Though everybody dies why die from eating? There is something in the food that captures children's taste and fast foods are generally set up in poor neighborhoods. Opinion? In those Inner cities, The amount is cheap and large. Importantly, while the poor gorge the modified version the rich return to organic which is what we in the so-called poor countries eat and took for granted. You know Mama, the rich countries succeeded in taking away our natural "livity," claiming that we are backward. They then turn around and give us their fat, while consuming -- their elite, that is -- our naturally organic food. They say we have it, but can't use it, and stupid as we can be, we believe. They use media to justify their superior nutrition flowing as it does with notions of pharmaceutical innovation, violence, conflict, crime and sexuality. Little did we know that backward food was advanced nutrition. Little did we know that without an abundance of fresh water soaked in our tongues, the mortality rate would've been higher.

In the days when our Mother shouted share, food did not contribute to sickness, Though it was believed that a banana eaten in the midday heat would hurt and could even kill. That was seldom the case. In fact, several methods were used to prevent the island's people from eating what the island produced, and from producing food other than a mono-crop. So much of what was called poisonous was at the heart of healing. Not only were poisonous stories passed on; the plants disappeared like many nutrient-filled fruits that they now seek to modify, or sell to us without seeds. Little did we know that the processing of noni was what mattered. Let us not underestimate the power of a foreign culture to sustain ignorance in a subject population by way of its own elite, its institutions, indeed its stories and modes of generating dark information and fear. Think carefully about the history of marijuana in our Caribbean societies! Think of it now. Everybody's on board!

Evil is a phenomenon in the psychic space of an island child. Its culture has an opposite built into its fertility. It can be reinforced by religion or advanced into science and art by prescribed knowledge. It is not always subsumed and may even be given greater attention without the knowledge of the attendants. Modern style and fashion can carry symbols of evil. It is in the heart of a young man who bullets another for his brand-coat. It is in the heart of an underground sex-trade employer who imports Third World women on the promise of a better life only to sex them into slavery. It is in the bomb. It is in the village woman who says to a Mother that her children will become nothing and steals their clothing to bury it with an animal's carcass. It is in the act of throwing scores of hot peppers on a church's steps as newlyweds emerge from it. It is in the serial killer's grin. It is aptly recorded when one attends an island's police day exhibition and discovers so many artifacts seized, artifacts used in the practice of necromancy. This was not the African diviner who still lived on island, whose ways had not been contaminated or pushed underground by early 20th century legislation. Her or his practice was different from the practice of evil. It was about healing not destruction and killing. What the police seized were artifacts of an evil trade even shadows of an evil. This brand was said to hurt maim destroy lives, if only the perceived victim could suggest it to self. Island occult practices?

In my home-town, stories raved about men who entered cemeteries to awake the dead seeking power to determine the outcome the outcome of a matter pending in the courts. Dabbling, they call it? Brave men calling Satan to a cemetery in Portsmouth, Dominica. Satan really has time, even for petty thieves. And what of those surrounding politicians who transform themselves into less than human creatures in the hope of keeping themselves in power? There is no doubt that principalities and powers in high religious and economic places have wreaked havoc in island communities. They carry very formal names and operate at the apex of developed and developing societies where consumption and compulsion are so phonetically close. Developed and developing? Is one stationary and the other in constant motion? We've been developing for so long, isn't it time that our Mothers deliver? And what of the developed? Can they be compassionate to those who're being formed, or are they eager, anxious to abort them? And what of those leaders opposed to abortion, but hungry to war, knowing clearly that war takes the lives of women and children? Compulsion to war? Then off course there is obsession. I am reminded that compulsion is physical and obsession is in the thought though one can have a compulsive obsession and an obsessive compulsion. Whichever way, suppliers are relentless, controlling thought and taste. Whichever way, the camera world is alive zooming and panning Mama.

CHAPTER 15

A Later Dream

A Catholic priest is on television talking about what happens after death. He humbly agrees that sociology, philosophy, theology and the entertainment industry cannot answer these questions. He acknowledges that he is going to have to be academic in clarifying his terms. He is about the business of finding a definition for Truth and settles for this: the conformity of the mind to reality. It is a view drawn from St. Thomas; he concedes. In addition to putting us in touch with reality, Truth, he contended, keeps us in touch with others. He concluded that Truth also delights and enlightens us. I listened intently, conscious of the non-print character of the text. It served as a great vehicle. I was traveling a mundane road with a subject that was not taken lightly or read with much gusto. But I had set my hand to the plough and the subject was pushing me to find expressions of love even in death. In whatever I encountered I saw the hope of lifting that dead connectivity, flowing from departure to return, from flesh to thought to feeling to weeping, and just beyond the cry of the soul, rejoicing. In the heart of mourning I heard laughter. I felt this abundant love for life and it was in such droves of plenty because of a promise which was excellent enough to present itself not only as a hereafter event but as happening now. Even the departed left lessons and impressions. Truth, the priest noted, keeps us in touch with others. He did not say whether the others had to be dead or alive to communicate to keep in touch. I can only assume the living though I know that our dead relatives do not like us to mourn to sorrow, frustration and anger. Ancient texts say this makes them sad. They want, they need us to build with confidence, great hope, strength, joy.

They say through visions and dreams, comfort yourself.

The Sun does not wait for you. Life is motion, compassion. Compassion? How does compassion work? Simply, it preserves its practitioner in its sun in the first place. Mama I heard the priest speak of the value in the process of keeping in touch. Touch as we know it may well be the surface of a larger domain in feeling. The priest implied the power of memory -- its living-on quality its coming to mind in waves after our loved ones have departed.

Four months after my Mother died I dreamt of her walking along a white-marbled pavement as if along sides of a pool. Even if she were dead, I was still thinking of her as blind -- the living being. She wore a seamless white, though it was as if torn with a few holes, appearing almost fashionable and ventilating. There was a spot along the walk-way which conveyed the impression of a drop to me and, I held my breath as she approached it only to realize that it was effect of light and shade. From then she was walking as if in flight. One of the most beautiful things happened: two or three children greeted her. She was very careful, I remember, not to step on their toes, not to trample them in any way. Don't know why I got up from the dream at that point. Through the dream I remembered her alive. It pleased me. It made a difference to my mourning.

CHAPTER 16

Inner Dialogue

Who was I the living to talk about death as if I had died before, seen its road signs, walked its streets and come to life again. Why did I in my youth ever think that I would not die. It must have been a streak of immortality. I laugh at the idea myself, one once labeled conceit, vanity.

It is life that I love, its earth-sites its vegetables, its fruits which convert so readily to flesh and blood, its water, its oceans its breath its dance its language every word. Was it St. Paul who said to live is Christ? There is something even more wonderful when he says to die is gain. It is not that we should long to die, but whenever it comes it is transformative, ascension. So many of these sayings have not been explored in the context of healing, psychological wellbeing. A burden, a stress as we say it, is lifted when you have the money to buy the house, food, clothes, the travel ticket. A burden is lifted when you have the money to cover the cost of education per semester, per year. It is lifted when you can visit the doctor, buy the medication. It is lifted when you have the means to an alternative treatment. Similarly, a burden is lifted when you're sure about your spiritual abode, or mental state. It is lifted when you recognize that your body is a gift, an energy house built for you free. This recognition is critical to a people coming out of a history of slavery and a violated body. To reconstitute such a body is to find what ophthalmology searches for mingled with the bodies entire tissue. It is to find trace beginnings of one original sound. It is to find awesome markers of ancient works knitting with perfection a structure, wonderfully wrought, too strong to have been subjected to such cowardice, such massive overdoses of fear. To approach the body as yours, knowing its content is not the only one of its kind, knowing it dates to a time that has not yet been identified beyond East Africa, is to encounter timelessness rising in your spit, on your tongue now, on your breath saying, yet not speaking English or any other lingua. Before spoken words defined us as human? It is inside the body that I go to listen to its ancient primordial silence, a little liquid running here and there, its heart doopdooping. When the women at Mother's house chanted hail Mary collectively, what happened? In their individual bodies were they encountering Mary, or the spirit of Mary? And if they did meet her in their bodies, what of her Son? And which sector, which of the systems of their bodies connected? Is it the blood, the endocrine system, the skeletal structure vibrating breath, muscle, nerve tissue, one neuron from the neurovascular site or something lighter beyond those within them? Was that communication outside boundaries of the cell, the gene, the DNA, the protein? If it is all flesh, then conduct surgery on the language emanating from its mouth. If it is all flesh and blood then give me a dictionary of that life filled with millions of words uttered over eighty-one years. Blood communicates. How is blood connected to, with blood though running under skin? How is my Caribbean blood, if I can call it thus, connected with, to that of a woman or man from China, Siberia, Nova Scotia, Connecticut, Nigeria, Kuwait, Peru, Indonesia, North West Territories, Alaska or Antigua? By way of culture? One thing is for sure: it is the same stuff, for one. Though they may speak of its types, it is the same. In that blood, breath roams freely collecting Life's history. And who can delineate this as its prescribed domain, draw lines imaginary or real, limiting its winged flight as if there were no other? It is by nature movement, in-dwelling and like sunlight, still boundless undying even in times of the famous disconnect. Where two or three are gathered, Mama used to say, God will grant their request. Surely blood has gathered. Certainly, there is heat, Fire in one body in motion -- so much so for two or three gathered in the same act of chanting Hail Mary, in Meditation or just plain conversation, moving words with atomic energy. Laughter, even laughter is contagious, surprising me in my own belly.

CHAPTER 17

Body so Vast

Surely, it would've pleased me more to write about my entire extended family. The "I" in the narrative has made me uncomfortable. Yet, I discovered that by pressing beyond the discomfort, by going into it, a spirit of renewal was waiting for me. It was good that discomfort arose. I became aware of how much I needed to know about my brothers and sisters. We could've connected more. I could not take that feeling for granted. It was an earth-cry instructing future relations. The spirit of redeeming took my attention. First, it was through me that hereditary traces of glaucoma first appeared and I became drunk with astonishment. Though my sisters Joycelyn, Pearl, and Eudora before she died, wore glasses, they had not been diagnosed as having glaucoma. Surprisingly, ten or so years after our Mother died, our brother Albert became borderline glaucoma and wore glasses. Since it was spotted early, laser was used to successfully open a flimsily-developing blockage over the trabecular meshwork. When it was identified in my eyes, those two ophthalmologists in Windsor, Ontario, did not think laser treatment. I would find out about its effectiveness when I moved to Toronto, but by then, the glaucoma, another claimed was far gone.

I had done some reading at college and universities, and with my Father's tutelage and astute guidance, diligently nourished life-saving seeds that he had sown subtly in my primary particles, my mind and soul. There was a boundlessness in my thinking -- a freedom that told me I could think whatever I wanted to think, say whatever I wanted to say. Thinking and saying began to become doing. Doing was responsibility, reward. In all this love for Thought and philosophy, my Mother's spirit was the anchor, the sober reality in everyday life. I vowed to unite them. Thus, when glaucoma broke its wings in my eyes, a spirit of perseverance and focus united with the search. I was the last place where my Mother thought glaucoma would have deposited its remains. It would surface in my brother Albert, only to be caught in its tracks in the eyes. He would go on to care meticulously for the other organs of his body because eyes were connected to liver, to stomach, in fact to all bringing light to all.

In her days before closure on the gene thing, she would express her deep regret to me that somehow between us a disorder had been communicated. There were times when she tried to say I am sorry. Her words faded into an apparent helplessness. I say tried because she did not speak it. Mothers deeper emotions are not expressed in words. She simply had to look at me, then her head would drop between her shoulders with that quiet smile screaming I hope you understand. you know, in flesh, surface is a satisfactory sign dimension. A clean skin may have been textured in pain as much as in thought. She smiles and screams. It's alright Mama. Truth, like silence screams Love.

If my brother Ernest were a writer he would have documented an incomparable biography of his Mother. He saw her each day. The same could be said of our sister Joycelyn, who came to know true value in patience, then finally, power in courage invested in her apparently from birth. I can well imagine that were my brother Albert a writer, he would capture all with his escape from the sneak thief narrative, even provide tools for making sure that it never returned!

For a few months after our Mother's transition, I realized, truly realized that there was much death in the world. My perception on living sharpened. Living was a second by second matter. In fact there was no time. There was no measure. This is it in agelessness, timelessness. This second beats with each universal other. I also noted that my Mother grew older gracefully like her Mother and grand-aunts who lived into their mid to late eighties. They lived. In those times, it wasn't the motif, you're here today, dead tomorrow. No. People lived and Life, Life figured in my childhood psyche as long.

Tell you, we eat well, but it was not all about food. We met and spoke with each other so often, encouraging, caring, supporting. It was a social environment of mutual care. This too ensures longevity.

When people died, they were not easily forgotten since whoever he or she was, their influence on the immediate community was memorable. I understand now why ancestors are so central to healing self, mind, healing community. But I, we need to understand it in terms of our remembering them and the effect of this healing process on body chemistry, in state of mind. Our bodies are certainly not just functions of a bio-chemistry; remembering as it does ancestral motifs, words, wisdom sayings, dances designs, planting secrets, modes of caring for self, methods of cooking, tested patterns of problem solution, response tendencies -- tell you, this is not exclusive property of flesh and bone.

I want to encourage the living to unite body mind and soul, gene, epigene, indeed cell and thought in living. I also want to open a discourse on visual impairment from an embodiment site and invariably, by way of Mama's sight-loss, her death and hope in the everlasting, infinite quality of life. I needed to record whatever I could remember, run with it wherever its tide tugged. Body was so vast, mind so boundless and to her, spirit eternal in Christ. The resurrection event was a lifting up out of death and thoughts of death -- believers are sure its power is with us now. How is this to be harnessed now for mind's flight, body's wellbeing, eyes seeing? Its energy is for all, though not known by the same name by a Muslim, a Hindu or Buddhist priest. What was this tradition and what does it say to the living who are dead inside. The dead inside, practitioners say, come to life. They (re)pent. They ask for (for)giveness for their sins. Truly, we're going to need studies connecting repentance, forgiveness and brain chemistry, their impact on mood change, on communication whether between cell and cell, consciousness and matter, or within oneself, rising early and laying in bed coursing through dreams manifests contents, the day's plans, yesterday's achievements, mistakes, smiles, or just with another human whose yeses are joyful, eyes full of energy, kindness, whose voice is patient, whose person, whose presence exhilarates. A spirit-filled energy? Now you can change diets and take up an exercise regime. You may laugh-read another line. There is that other dimension not visible that touches you, moves you to contemplation and prayer drops you to your knees or brings you tears of joy like victory. Clearly, my Mother's death became a point of entry or departure for my discourse. For sure, she did not want me dead. No matter where I emerged, body mind and spirit had to be alive. The discourse had to be living despite the fact that it surfaced from a departure a death a breath that had left what was one of its dwelling places for over eight decades. She so enjoyed living that I had to salvage her life-bits in all this going forward. In many ways, we were obliged to find life not only in the hereafter but now. Her sheer physical strength at eighty years told us that there was more than just the body here. We had to receive the Fire knocking at our bones. Other than the Fire of the gospel that Neville brothers of Louisiana sang about, the one at Pentecost, you know the one of tongues, those we lit in camps or even those emanating from acts of the oppressed, Fire is not something we play with. Other than in sexual passion it was rare to find Fire in the body being part of everyday talk. We knew living, active energy in joint, marrow and blood but a consuming fire?

CHAPTER 18

Strength in That Eternal Deposit

African collective unconscious manifesting in the Caribbean saw fire in its pool of archetypes as permeating all movement, all mobility. Those who came to Haiti, Jamaica, Grenada, Barbados, those who came, all carried universal Fire in their bosoms clearly interpreted differently from the Fire-power of gun-powder. This was Fire in spirit, giving Life to Life. Their very digestive tract's fire consumed what they were fed in measured amounts, surviving each rotting piece each fresh addition. Fire? They had what we call an instinct for the word that became. That flesh would be subject to beatings. Those whose guns came in search of human bodies to enslave had to be savages, were bound to be evil. Do they truly know value in form? Did they know this was a spiritual being having a human experience? You know, forgiveness is in order particularly when one considers that a universal sacrifice was made "once for all." Still, that body continues to be subject to the gene thing. The sacrifice did not eclipse the issue running in families. Maybe we are of the same family as the crucified. My Mother would've been wary of the process of this Henry discourse and where it was heading but

I am about filling that empty blind spot contributing to correcting a human evolutionary error.

A question comes to mind. It regards a section of humanity known as the wicked. How long Lord, Mama lamented, How long shall the wicked "prosper." They could be anyone, from a corrupt government, a class or a business community. They could even be among the poor themselves, who pray for release from their neighbor's ways seen as wicked. They cry out, whoever they are who're suffering, Lord how long. The Lord seems to know the time. In fact the Lord knows how long those wicked will prosper for. Even I feel them running. Tell you, angels buzzed, this could be for a long, long time. In this time, the oppressed lose many generations while the wicked prosper under the eyes of Heaven. Who was/is wicked? Is it this text and its drumming voices? Was it a modern, a slave-driver, a capitalist, a slave-ship's captain, an invading army, a planter who worked his chattel to daylight and prays at the chapel before setting the day's quota. Who says who's wicked. Those who sell arms or those who are killed by them. The wicked and their generations prosper while the good at heart lose several generations before the promise of liberation comes to their stock exchange and local pharmacy. I hear the propagated idea that abundance is in the hereafter. Maybe this is truer than I want to believe, but living is where I am and living is "who" I'm interested in. I hope a generation advances without fear, the discourse that the price was paid unfairly because it was paid twice: on the cross and on the plantation.

My Mother's death became my discourse. It showed me that it is brave to write from good. Good is the unexplored. It is the frontier without end. It is the nothing zone where I become the medium to utterances that fill without causing illness that support without seeking reward that accompany a stretching hand without seeking return that takes the time to say thank you. So I come into my Mother's domain to find her body and its symbolic existence on Earth. What did she achieve? How does what she intercepted inform me? Jesus Christ was, is, and never will be about injustice. I really wonder how the Son of Man stomachs the injustice of man to man. The word stomachs is my

Mother's. Even when we do not know this answer we choose justice. Every religious movement and institution under the Sun knows God is love. It is not easy to construct a discourse out of the fields of love. It is easy to hate. To write about the relationship between my Mother and I while she was alive and now as she returns to her Maker is therefore, to do justice to her religious and spiritual experience rooted, planted in Love. Even when I do not immediately understand it, I do not want to judge it. I want to learn from it take what she hands me, run with it, leap, hurdle to find new ways of giving and giving life to life remembering that spirit of the living God is in it and in my brothers and sisters and children, in the very ground where she is laid, all that is around it, the town, its people good and evil, its global community, nation, its trees, their leaves and youth laughter. And, I ask, is it just good and evil? Is it all about sin? Where is eternity moving my heart, breathing my lungs, feeding my alveoli, my villi, cleansing this liver, seeing, hearing, speaking, touching, walking with me, with us? What is it that is not taught about this eternity, deposited, paid for and living in bone, blood, breath, muscular strength, emotional intelligence, even potency, reproductive fertility. It is in thought's speed, wise expression, knowing keys to favor and sounds of abundance. Is it not? Even in the worst of times, women of my Mother's generation stood their ground. I could hear my Mother saying, the spirit of the living God can let me go but I'm holding on to this garment of light. I can hear her saying I'm going through the darkest pit but I'm holding on. I can barely see my hand as I lift it to my mouth. Sorrow eats me. Helplessness swirls. I'm not letting go. You may choose not to answer me, I'm not letting go. I am hungry. I'm not letting go. I am driven into lonely fields, dry places, bitter streams. I am not letting go. Day in day out I rise to the same visual tightness, the same veil, the same darkness. I am not letting go. You may walk passed me and my brothers and sisters while we wail on our knees. I am not letting go. All around us there seems to be no hope. I am not letting go. Step by step. Step by step. We've come from far and you will not receive us in our chains and under our brands. But we're not letting go. Melt into the crowd if you wish. I'm not letting go. You're with me and you know I can make you strong. I will scream at you if I have to, burst down high gates if I have to. I am not letting go. You are justice and it's time to flow. We've been running, dragging, stumbling, crossing waters, blistering heat has scorched us, but justice. Justice has not come materially, physically, legally. Ingratitude? Should we be satisfied with one quarter of our reward? No. This is not our abundance. And many times, sometimes, just when we think the trickle bursting to flood, weather changes. When will the highway be clear? Are we born to carry suffering; one of humanities species? No. This is not being rude. Too many of us do not know your joy, not because we do not love you or render your heart's strengthening. Debatable eh? Yes. If you're loved you do not suffer, those detractors shout. They carry ammunition and influence. We weigh loss while prices rise in market places. We're holding on. We're holding on and you know it.

These people were amazingly powerful, muttering, humming, "come by here Lord/come by here." They barely had sleeping space. They spoke, sang, hummed as if this Lord was someone far, whom they had to call into their presence. Their call drew a response; this is communication between dancer and drummer. The second phase was being the being called, a sort of possession, belonging to the time, the leaps into timeless thought, Lord! The spirit of this Lord rose out of their bellies. They'd rock, sway, leap in body and mind as its universal energy thickened, wrapping their brain. The air became charged synchronously. Presence. We need this technology in these fabricated times. Blacks Brain Territory is unknown, is eco-property governed by laws not recognized or known by governments, especially White ones! We are in the whirlwind, in consuming fire. We are connected under this new communication covenant, laws written and inscribed in our hearts and minds as active property. It is our time and our people are returning in our children this time with knowledge and power In the Spirit! We shall see returning priests arch-bishops and bishops politicians professors MBAs agriculturists geologists farmers fishermen nurses teachers lawyers musicians painters playwrights acrobats gymnasts netballers footballers actors actresses engineers athletes accountants architects seers diviners sea captains pilots doctors healers entrepreneurs merchants hoteliers environmentalists foresters food technologists technicians computer analysts masons joiners designers tailors seamstresses entertainers therapists dentists nutritionists police officers soldiers bankers dreamers economists physicists chemists biologists magistrates pharmacologists florists restauranteurs broadcast-journalists hair stylists cosmetologists small business people hucksters historians philosophers poets dramatists midwives.

Let's uphold sense of history -- another sense to be added to the five or the millions you already are experiencing in this restored relation with ancestry. They have come again only this time you are blessed, you are moved, pre-programmed to be positive like the mind's galactic direction. Who has scattered your brain, taken from you the fine tradition that brought together Africa Asia Europe America, stream, rock. A fecund information age replaces a historically alienated God with an ever-present strength more so in those who've always known. Sunburnt people have always known God, an absurdity to those who never received others with thanks. Though sprouting in foggy habitats, this marks an inevitable bursting forth of the creative imagination, a renewal call, a Caribbean redemption song! Intelligences are "coming in from the cold" breaking nuts in mist as they come in to fire our eyes -- those seeing yesterday, today, tomorrow clear! It marks the return this time of the eternal and everlasting. It may be a wilderness voice. It may be the voice of many angry waters still communicating that all will be moved and changed. In truth and beauty, it is the sudden heart-skip, dried lips on fire in utterances, calm palms, acute nostrils, dog's best-friend ears, warm, strong hands, legs, ready to flight, jump, stand for justice fuming fast out of Earth. It is too, a dream of a coherent neurological system, a magnificently functioning brain lit in its search at the mouth of a cave overlooking a pebbled beach, approached by way of a green path. It is visioning. I think that the Chinese body, like any other, will discover that it is stringed by more than thousands of meridian points-- the human body is detailed electricity. Indeed, interconnectedness, communication depicts the human form --even over distance and between old and young, Red and White, Black and Yellow, Blue and Indigo living and dead, energy is exchanged. Cure and healing have arrived! Hallelujah!

CHAPTER 19

Glaucoma, the Last Thing

Listen. I was resting the afternoon our brother called to say Mama had died. Somewhere between sleep and wake I received a vision of her with both her eyes open blue and red-ringed. This goes beyond race. A darkened spot separated the two in a third or first eye position -- depends on who's seeing -- and extended over the nostril's bridge. Unlike my daughter Roberta, I had not developed the skill of controlling or determining the course of the dream. I sprang out losing contact and communication with that powerful figure. She had those eyes which looked straight at you, at me whenever they focused. As the glaucoma progressed and an apparent veil of mucus thickened she tended to look upward as if the unclouded remaining spaces were in the lower section of the eyes. By forty-seven much of my right eye was covered by a dark veil or cloud. Bob Marley had sung "come take the veil from off your eyes." This was a call to depart from ignorance. I had to move beyond this physical hold-up. My patience is not as infinite as hers -- I am asking questions when she would have chosen to remain silent, carrying instead the Fire involved in coping with a dread. I could take her stance and see this as my lot with no solution except that which is partial and reduced intensively almost scientifically to the interior of the eyes. When I say intensively I speak of the reductionism known traditionally to be functional in the sciences. Glaucoma could not be restricted to the eye in and of itself. As long as glaucoma continues to be treated exclusively in the eye, chances of finding a cure remain futile -- mere responses to approved theory.

I did not know of glaucoma until it struck me and then my Mother revealed that was what they called hers. Mother did not wear her visual impairment as if it were a problem; watching her one would never say she was having difficulty seeing up to the latter years of her sixtieth birthday. I am to this day, haunted by the fact that her disorder did not take my attention not even after those MDs had discovered it in me. I was thirty-four and at a Canadian university. I had spent a wonderful semester reading molecular genetics and was thrilled by the ease with which the ideas spawned in this science came to me. Had I known; I might have minored in Biology. Thing is, when I left my Mother's house at twenty-two, she was fifty-six. By the time I left for university, she was sixty-six, already feeling, experiencing the impact of Glaucoma but she did not show it. She used drops, yes, but not one of us thought of blindness, not even she. The knowledge that glaucoma was a leading cause of blindness might have been mentioned to her, but I gather she must have thought she could beat it.

In filling out doctor's documents she would have had to state who in her family was visually impaired. It was by way of her father. Was she warned that her children could be affected? The gene thing was not popular then, though it was community lore to state that his or her Father or Mother had such and such and so it was not unusual that he or she had it, or had died from it. When I returned from university five years later, I observed that something was wrong, but still, I did not move quickly to research glaucoma. When I told her that it had been diagnosed in me, she then revealed that this was what she had. I smelt the coffee before I woke up. She kept me out and I did not resist. I did not crash down the gates. I should've identified the problem and moved to solve it. I did not have to be asked to find a solution. It is a powerful lesson.

Blindness was the last thing on my mind. It is now the first thing to be acknowledged, opened up, understood, unveiled. How suddenly and in microcosm the last becomes the first!

CHAPTER 20

Need and Race for a Cure

Disease is truly a great war strategist striking in the least expected area. Disease travels long in the back-streets and alleys of that marvelous city known as the human body. Long before it appears in the capital there is a sense of imbalance. Since subjectivities are not deemed medically correct they are not communicated. They do not constitute fact, are not objective and so teach nothing. The city is therefore less offensive on account of their exclusion policies.

Dogs are known to signal the coming storm, birds fly in frequent collective formation, children grow restless. The body talks. Changes begin on an all clear day with no sign or feeling of dread. They clandestinely avoid detection exhibiting random pockets of symptomatic, almost invisible attacks often disregarded by the clock-bound modern. It has been this way for long.

New York's National Association for the Visually Handicapped (NAVH) was quite clear that in 1954, little was available or understood about the visually impaired. The project is not much older than the rise of the Civil Rights Movement. Its achievements are to be applauded. But understanding visual impairment seemed never to have included and adopted initially, the cure motif. True, assistive technology is increasing its software diversity, though the eye in itself remains the concentrated zone of disorder. Moreover, it appears that in ophthalmology little time is allocated to advancing fresh theoretical approaches to combat anticipated increases in visual impairment -- approaches acknowledging the integrated nature of the human body. Assistive technology software diversity will not be the answer to how environmental or diurnal changes play on the visual system. The same National Association for the Visually Handicapped, contends that by 2020, forty-three million Americans will have some form of visual impairment. It appears to me that visual impairment is a non-visual phenomenon, and those who are thus impaired tend generally to replicate sayings of those searching the eyes to treat them. Ophthalmologists need listen to patients describe their symptoms. There's knowledge there for ophthalmology's growth -- the eye is not restricted to the head. What was even worse in 54, according to NAVH, was that few really cared. Imagine how blindness, visual impairment was regarded and carried in New York in those 50s. What did he/she do wrong? Interestingly, there are groups in the southern United States and worldwide, who believe that blindness is caused by an affliction. Indeed, visual disorder today is a least urgent matter compared to AIDS/ HIV cancer heart disease autism, obesity. African-Americans had better come together to deal with glaucoma because Caucasians are wrestling with macular degeneration. The literature describes it as "age related". It is a preoccupation, one in which central or peripheral loss is significant to research, but one which barely matters to the patient. Whites lose it this way and Blacks lose it that way. It's the same eye when it carries a disorder. Those who treat the eyes, seldom know disorders of the eyes. Well, not really. One is blue, the other is black, brown. Colors? Wait till the sixth chakra flashes its colors. Then off course, since they treat surfaces, there is room for technology, assistive technology. The body is negated. The deaf are given aids. The speech impaired are using signs. The physically handicapped take wheelchairs. Lots of helpful, intelligently manufactured technology. Doctors from both the Hippocratic and Integrated medical traditions often agree, in principle at least, that in addition to those intelligent bits and extensions, the body needs internal support whether biochemical by way of nutrition, solidly developed stress comprehension techniques, tension release intervention methods, the formal adoption and acceptance of acupuncture, and the inclusion of herbal medicine. The question remains, what cures these days, really cures? What did Christ Jesus use to cause the speech impaired to speak, or what would he have used today to bring those living with autism to full maturity and balance? What energy was it that flowed into the feet of the paraplegic? Why doesn't science acquaint itself with such technique, such technology? We go to Mars and the deepest oceans and forests by day and night in light and darkness. We manufacture invisible soldiers. Those coming out of my Father's reflections, indicate that scientists, doctors of medicine, think that such healing methods, those used by Christ, require too much energy. Surely, technology has progressed, while the purpose of medical knowledge is in question. Furthermore, flesh has become weaker, unable to conduct, eager to cost its time, its very training limits. Bodies are media to business and knowing. There is in knowing however, implications of connectivity which are not applied to the business of curing bodies. More than ever, after prescriptions are written the matter is over until the next visit, the next refill. Where is the medicine that never has us coming back? I gather, hidden in physicians knowledge. Why repress, suppress it? Knowledge cannot, will not be repressed when it is truth. Knowledge that is suppressed, though developed originally from a relationship with the body, its inner spaces of intelligence and its patterns of emotions, surely breaks forth, cognitively, institutionally. Structures crumble as it rises. The court is moved as it speaks its just position. Medicine is going to have to embrace compassion, not as religious requirement, but as spiritual visitor, one coming to stay, one asked to.

There is a screaming need for cure echoing across vast gatherings of narcissistic techno humanity -- absurd as it may sound -- while mercy's slipping its files into our consciousness into our bodies. Too much energy eh? Ophthalmologists will not call on nutritionists, massage therapists, naturopathic and homeopathic practitioners or acupuncturists to jointly build and support a cure regime. Profits have to be shared and ophthalmology is lucrative business. In 2002, 2.5 (milliliters of Xalatan sold in my island for EC$120. My last visit to a doctor in Atlanta in 2007 cost US$125, and you know it's only five minutes per patient -- the gaze has constructed patterns. It does not have to search too long. It's hand just prescribes. It is worth knowing that when I left Dominica in 2002, Cusopt and Xalatan were the leading drugs for treating intraocular pressure. When I visited the best ophthalmologist in Atlanta in 2007 (having moved from a developing to a developed society), he told me they were still the leading drugs of choice. Glaucoma in the 70s? What a trip! What a faith walk!

By her 75th birthday our Mother was diagnosed as borderline diabetic but twenty years before, that is in the 70s, I was not aware of any publicized connection being made in the islands health sector between diabetes and blindness. Diabetes was called sugar and the numbers were few. Diabetes and high blood-pressure took off in large measure in the 80s and peaked in the late 90s. Eighties dietary change must have contributed to the borderline factor. Though people eat and eat enough, no explicit connection was made between what one eat and disease. Even after our natural living achievements in the 70s, a dominant colonial education instruction stressed eggs, milk, cheese, meat, beans. Today in the US, dairy is suspect. In spite of tutelage, we called all animal flesh meat and all beans, peas. Eggs came from our fowls; each person had a few hens and one or two cocks. Yes, two. Milk came from cows, even goats, and was sold in community, not bought in supermarkets. A pea tree could be found blossoming -- we bought lentils and red beans. In those days, they were beans. Fruits which poured abundantly out of the land, when eaten at school breaks, disappeared into our mouths as if under military control. We had to line up for a banana. I think they tried, but when it came to fruits we consumed out of school, they failed. We were true rebels, ripping the snake out of the ripened banana bunch, the one that had fallen to the ground, beautifully candy, sweet indeed for a kouwez to rest in. Little did you know; Eve's friend loves natural candy, loves the purity in Mother's milk. But this is another matter, another sailorman's mythology on a night when nature's moon reigns resplendent on water.

In the days when we sought our own fruit, water was fresh, real fresh and flowed abundantly, truly flowed down from Zion. The Sea was our hospital -- curing everything from insomnia to sore-eyes. In those mid-sixties we were not talking about life-style diseases; today, a perfect reflection of modern culture, its diet its tensions and dysfunctions.

CHAPTER 21

Silent Cultivators of Ideas

So when my Mother asked that I forget about the gene thing, I realized that she must be acquainted with an aspect of our physical constitution and early living, holding the capacity to overcome this bio-chemical explanation for disease, no matter how plausible and valid its representation, no matter her limited grasp of its diagnostic methodology, its science. She needed me to understand that this glaucoma could be and had to be overcome. I could look to stem-cell research, a combination of traditional and modern medicine bolstered by that inner journey in a world of boundless information and prayer, the lifting of the veil in the Holy of Holies the revisiting of the body and blood with new eyes. Stem cells? When will the costs drop like a fruit to the blind? She had prayed and died blind. She had walked seven hundred fifty miles of the one thousand. I thought she had failed.

You know in many island societies, Becoming something meant success within the public domain. Those silent cultivators of home economy and industry who showed up each day on time for forty years, obeyed authority without flinching, nurtured their children and relations with their neighbors, did not become? Actually these women worked the fields, serviced small retail businesses, ran their homes, shipped agricultural products for sale to other islands and took to sea as part-time or full-time hucksters. Their prayers are on the ocean floor their patience in the wind. They visualized for their children on water. They exhaled. it's amazing how death makes us equal. I only had to walk the remaining two hundred fifty!

In the externalizing world of my youth I could not see the wonder in Mother's movement. I did not think that she too needed love. She gave so freely. She seemed to have an overflowing cup. Later in my adult life I discovered that to give love to her was to find mine strengthened. In real life, love is instant in effect, just like pure medicines. It was this inner strength that I needed to harness, bring into perfect use from the abundance of its infinite possibilities -- to borrow a phrase from Ayurveda. It is this inner woman and man or just this man and woman that medicine is about to learn from.

CHAPTER 22

The Runs in Families Business

In the newly-emerging 80s health culture she was at the level of the pill Diamox, to the point where she fell asleep. It was one of those big round chalk-white pill that just doped her. Remember alertness shines through the eyes. I recall those bottles of Timolol and Pilocarpine as they replaced Diamox. She applied them with so much clinical assurance, with a religiosity outstripping her dogma. If those eye drops cured -- and she believed with all her heart that they could -- she would have been cured after seven months so consistent and structured was her application. I never thought of her becoming hard of seeing and she, she believed almost to the end that her sight would be restored. She trusted the medication would work, not knowing at that time, that the medication was not pure medicine -- it was not designed to cure. I believe she resolved herself to herself when she began to forget her range of psalms and scriptures. But you know in the midst of cognitive disappearances, there are always appearances.

I remember playing the guitar while she sang with me "have thine own way Lord/have thine own way." When I thought the chorus was all, she took to singing the verse, and turned sharply in my direction when I held a wrong chord! Hearing is generally excellent in the visually impaired and if I was going to present a song to Mama, one asking the Lord to have thine own way, I had to have practiced it well. Take nothing for granted Stein. Take nothing for granted.

Off course she had eye surgery and it barely made a difference. She prayed to the point of weeping. Her eyes showed no signs of improvement. The people before believed, and people today believe too that surgery marked the beginning of the end of the disease. And it can be the end. But I think it's who you are. I think it's also who and what you know. The head of Johns Hopkins department of Pediatrics was diagnosed as having prostate cancer. He selected the best surgeon and was cured. And he used the word "cured" in the Larry King interview. Ben Carson's' faith in the Lord Jesus Christ is also well represented in his mini-autobiography titled "Healing Hands." He is a neuro-surgeon and man of prayer. He believes in the actual coming into being of the spirit of the living God into human affairs, even academia, scholarship and intellectual performance. He knows intimately the subtle chemistry of a neuron. Indeed, he is closely engaged in the business of God's microcosmic representation in the body and still unlike many reductionists, has the power to speak of the love of God in Christ Jesus. His cure was secured. Truly he knew the best. He depended on a quality of technology -- a know-how that was physical, material, cognitive, intellectual, spiritual. He had the best of both worlds, even those in between!.

Undoubtedly, many have benefited from the work of exceptionally gifted men and women. We did not have such luxury. Eyes remain a mystery oracle. She fasted and it did not matter. She became angry and it did not matter. Within the last five to seven years of her life she seemed to be coming to terms with the dreaded inevitable but not without anger, physical strength and a sort of resolve that this thief had to be caught.

Supposedly, there's an energy space a life force in me a small parcel of life that has its own life apart from me, the conscious thinking person. Mama, based on the way ophthalmologists behave, not even God knows this place. It is genetic hereditary. It cannot be visited.

It cannot be reached not even by God's measuring line and light. It runs in families. The Creator does not know its genesis, its origin. It is mystery even to the maker of the body. Strange, is it not? Sound will not reach it. In truth, only it can reach itself and that itself is not itself. They scramble, those who've come upon the Twenty-First Century twist to this micro-skeleton that lives in every family -- an impossible thorn to remove to rip. No one seems to know where or when it began and no effort will be made to stop it because, that they claim, is impossible. Prayer they say will not stop its march. Fasting will not dissipate this determined tornado. It lives in me not as a vital force but as a disease-causing agent. It is "badder" than the best agents carrying the highest technology: anciency, family history, rulers and kings proclivities, queens fornications. I would have to say so. It has to be "badder;" it carries only disease. But it seems to reach back in time up to a point. We shall begin with macular; they proclaim. We have found the gene -- receptors therein respond effectively. It sounded as if they were probing and hit a rock that carried a peculiar sonar vibration. We did not go in search of the macular gene; we simply came upon its jelly. Loss of central vision is our priority though and will remain our priority for the next five decades. Research on the glaucoma gene is still largely unfunded, but we must stress, just as significant. The macular gene is not the glaucoma gene. Liver cells laugh. Heia, I laugh too! There's a dark cloud outside the window of the soul. The priest does not know the intricate dance the geneticist has identified. The choreographer's memory will not plumb its dark interconnect -- the diviner, the diviner is not acquainted with microscopia. To remove it from families, specialists say, we must grow back in time, but let us not incorporate timelessness. Doesn't make sense. My Mother's dead, her Mother and Father are too. Their grandparents are already saints bought by a trader from the house of the immortal! Runs in families eh? It defies my history. It seems not to be of my race. It shows no regard for my circumstance. It does not read the present. It bears symptoms with no cause diseases with no cure, thoughts with no spirit, no soul, the body with no mind no connection no. It is a deadly sentence for the innocent. They've inherited. Maybe it's an attempt to positivize inherited flesh and blood traits. So we vibrate, restore ancestral thought. We restore the body -- we take it from the grave of this world system through knowledge and power in the spirit of the living God we restore. We?

When my Fathers prints appear on my brow they should be applauded by silver-haired elders who notice. Not for one moment should I be permitted to feel in community that traces of Father in me are ominous. Too many cultures fear the rising up of the Son in the image of the Father and vice versa. Still, beneath the skin behind the skull in the quiet movement in the walking feet Mama struts with her XX. Genetics? Within Papa's presence is the smile that no one sees; larger eyes seeking to forgive gentler hands hoping you understand power of pleasure over pain healing over killing. Behind the invisible Mother is a world of many faces those dead and alive. The dead are alive here. They emerge so clearly and go under like the Sun!

You know, as a child I use to think that the Sun went into the Sea. All of life must have come from the Sea because it is so vast. It seems the only place to bring forth this genetic diversity. The Sun will not enter into it. The Sun is farther. These faces rise from Sea to Sun, that is. from Earth to parts of Heaven. And what if Earth is already in Heaven? Its people may well be asleep: they don't seem to know it is! Let's play. What if the end of the sea was also the end of the Sun. This does not make sense. The Sun is at the center of our galaxy which is outside another, that is inside another, that is between another and another they're just discovering, addressing with their optics, announcing, we have reached the possible end of the universe. Mars, with a breath of full curiosity rocks a little. The Sun snarls flares; Venus sweats. All on Earth wonder. Red is chosen. Psychic phenomenon tinkles in a tea-cup in Siberia, in back-streets of Moscow. Billionaires practice visually guiding stocks. Markets and Mars? What I know? Does not matter to a returning spirit or to billions and billions and billions of faces that have departed their skeletons micro on Earth or left their ashes on the banks of the Ganges. I play. It is my Mother Milky Way. They've found a parallel, they've found a parallel breasted universe, and its Mother, its female. What do we do now when this Mother comes to embrace us, swallow us into her womb again to cast us, cast us with eagle's love down the flight of a third and fourth and ourselves? What shall we do patriarchy? Never mind. Let yourself loose. Relax. I'm playing in the sky, me and water swinging and not falling. We shake the tree. Mangoes fall to the Earth. Wonder if they could fall passed Earth and hit the Sun? Silly fool. What would we not have done if we could throw objects at the Sun. You know, a male or female Lexus, a space-raft, ship along an ocean of air that thins. I'm going in. Are you coming? You know I do not mean this coming that your smile steals from red-hot Mars to flirt with Venus. Are you coming? There's music here. Food. You know fresh banana, kouliw, cabbage, christophene trying to touch protein. Play a little. Loosen your imagination. That's what screws are for. Cell pounds to a shell, a conch softened to chewing. Co K. Don't laugh. That's what cell and cell do, Thought, mood. I tried to enter(tain). You don't want to? You don't want to eat? Music then. Good for your soul. Dinner and then the African Ensemble. Come on. It is my Mother's concert hall, her play, her song. Look at the torches still dripping lagli. My Father use to tell her he wanted his dead body burnt. Mere ashes? she inquired: what will we say to the audience when you are gone; that you were once a man of great interest, quite male, exceptionally good kisser, great help, rebel, dancer, player in politics, dramatic war theorist? What shall we say? That genetically you carried the XY of righteousness? Delighting in a lovers moment? From this spot where she sits against a banana tree, cool breeze fondling her genetic nappy, whole texts open in the wind, whole texts on happiness and glacial geology. What happened to Fire. He asked. Consumed in Fire. What was he thinking? Earth is a mere grain? Nah. In the beginning, God created the Heavens and Earth. Who made Mars? That's the Heavens. Don't make me laugh. Co K? I tried again. You know, Earth like the first human was void and without form until light and breath. You're breaking roots. What happened to the African Ensemble? Xylophones in Heaven? Angels in this ensemble? You're adding to the Word. Mere dust to dust. Ashes to ashes.

CHAPTER 23

Medical Schools Paradigms Shifting

These people had a desire, sipping now into the body of this narrative. What weights. Truth is every family race tribe carries its bag of curses. The more I understood this, the more I realized I am, was, will be a representative of my kind. I began to get an idea a sense, albeit partially of the general course of life. I began to feel that my life was not mine but that of some people who lived long before me, whose deeds continue to curse or bless me while advancing the course of discernment, even someone else's agenda wherein I served merely as a pawn on this board of dualities. As a child of the 50s I measure it as too heavy. Beyond veils of another's agenda? Maybe. Maybe it is eternity looking sweetly at temporality showing me a detailed picture in picture. Maybe the promise and the reality are at work in human form with the reality receiving greater everyday attention while the promise gracefully seeks out prepared vessels.

I seek to invest healing, insight, restoration and creativity in the Caribbean body walking gently having been cautioned by rumbling thunderous rebellion and a thirst for justice held as priority. It is heavy and it is light. I cannot fail in believing knowledge springing from the ground at the Oval! Stream of consciousness, this must be Bouyon's aromatic madness! It springs from the shores of bauxite planes, from the smell in spices and timber, natural gas and steel, water and teeming life in pools along narrow paths where fruit seeds sprout and caterpillars still unfold in Wind. I reach out to her spirit with true ancestral alacrity, adulation. From Wind she whispers on our behalf. Her flesh and blood dissipating in the Portsmouth Catholic cemetery could not speak to utter words touching its melted constitution. From within its marrow, it communicates years of standing, a specific dietary and chewing pattern, a pastoral lifestyle a protein content, sunshine water, feet that had walked long, teeth deep in gum. Pelvic bones may as well convey traces of eight children as they're balanced and breaking loose. Language here is silence, a representation of someone, a congregation an assembly tonguing their breaths singing she was here she passed here leaving this hardening substance. It is however to the final breath she gave up, the one she inhaled at birth that I address my plea -- returning again to the heart. This latter, this tissued habitat is crucial; I read green things here, things not written in books, whole texts engraved, deposited, thought out, text appearing, disappearing. All was not available to immediate memory not each line, not each quote, date, quantity. Something stayed however, something retrieved through reflection, thinking, thought clinging to thought, language stringing language, dream reviews, conversations, social interactions. I would learn about short, medium and long-term memory, chunking, use of images, objects and patterns facilitating recall. I enjoyed intuition; the faith element entailed in constructing a sentence not knowing the complete thought but pursuing it anyway. Where were they stored? In what form? I suspect a pattern of emotions, the much-loved dancer's muscle pitching out step after step until the irregular becomes fluid. In this fluent state, short, medium and long-term embraced each other; strings of thought knew themselves and another form, shape of themselves. If they had eyes, they would see this other apart from themselves, yet connected to their seeing, their stringing, their shifting chord formations.

Over and above this psychologizing, I needed strength of spirit. I needed strength of spirit to go on despite a training, a background screaming too frequently where is objectivity. It was an extremely important question, one acknowledging that it too is subject to selection, memorizing. This may well be virtues in and of a rational mind. I share the view though I could not partake of it at this particular event. I thought: there must be something written like this before. The language of return like that of exile or resistance burns from a candlestick of a fine, accessible tradition. I chose to settle for the form I understood: skull rib pelvis shoulder bones. I cared about the becoming rather than the naming. Plants animals micro-organisms have more exact names. It did not always matter as long as they served as media to what I was feeling and wanted to express from thought process. I often thought how beautiful it might have been to talk about protozoa, or chemistry of water as it leached from territory to graveyard aqueous humor and anterior chamber to temporal lobe. Sense of smell never seemed to figure and if I said what I smelled many may not believe.

When I revisited my Mother's grave site a few days after she was buried a wonderful aroma a natural perfume greeted me. As I struggled to connect land I see, I became aware that the impact of the recently buried body on its physical surrounding was of interest. Strange? I wondered whether churches believed some thing percolated. There was movement -- like Wind we smell the Spirit. The language and communication of the microcosmic began to thrill me just as the body's aromatic healing ecology, spiritual well-being, communication with God and my fellow human. I became increasingly aware of interdependencies. The interactionalities of water and land-forms held my attention. What when a human body lies between land forms, hydrogen and oxygen mixed? You know in this mourning situation; I was thinking of so many scenarios! Could that aroma have been my perception? Does coming to know have a redolence? Is knowledge living in the Wind, its blown pollen? Aquatic life and land life? Land, dead human life, tree-trunk expansion? It is well researched, just as that relation existing between salmon nitrogen isotopes and the structure of hemlock trees in Northern British Columbia. I thank Canadian geneticist David Suzuki for his brilliant television documentary on the intricate association. Fish and tree-trunk sap? Suzuki found that tree-rings increased in size as a result of salmon decay at their roots. Should not surprise therefore when I say I came upon this documentary while writing Returns, feeling synchronicity in its very appearance on screen. What does not bring life to life? Curing? Medical schools are going to have to look outside, even inside their centuries-old body map, inside a spiritual mind's geography where fish bone minerals and cambium teach nature relations, indeed, wherein they teach nature's stringy language.

CHAPTER 24

Traces of Disability Languaging

This narrative is at one point technical at another ecopsychologic and, ecopoetic on death expanding the reduced to general living, daring on account of the fact that I'm writing about my Mother to telescope Networks such as families races nations largely on my understanding of issues shared during conversations with her. She would not be thoroughly acquainted with the boundaries I cross or do not enter signs being violated. Many are present world scenarios -- the ecological, the rise of police states in democracies and what one Columbia University professor called the privatization of violence. This is my time that her inner universal vision spotted cited, sparked, but was not overtly stated. Memory deposits? No matter how raw, how crude, they elicited legally from cultivated property. They knew and practiced the organic in agriculture as well as in language.

My Mother's people, her blood brother, cousins, aunts, uncles, nieces and nephews had an organic relation with Old Testament language and concepts. They understood structure: phonetically the word earned a nuance, accompanied by facial and bodily communication -- semantically it seemed the speakers had experienced the word in action and knew that action attitude or behavior from the moment it emerged. Their usage can baffle a naming or noun society. I had to search for the meaning of lickerish, used as an adjective. It means, lecherous; lustful; lewd, greedy or eager. "She too lickerish," I'd hear my Mother say. Interesting. The word reproachful took time to settle into meaning. Was this about blaming? Then there was covetous and worthless. Finally there was begrudging which meant many things, among these being feelings of ill will or resentment at the possession or employment of (something) by another; giving with ill will or reluctance etcetera. What was instructive about the use of this word, is that it issued as saying to be understood by the speaker whose meaning was validated in the body language speaking with it. Inadvertently, they understood greed and the deadly sting of jealousy. Mama warned her children against envy and counseled us on the limits of vanity and conceit. In political linguistics, these would be treated as concepts bearing as they do the tango of internal contradictions. We grasped the line in their utterance internalizing all implications in one shot!

Ambition made sense in their days. Remember when Shakespeare called ambition vain? To those of Mama's generation coming into adulthood during the rise of Hitler it seemed clear as he forayed into Siberia. They knew what it meant when someone was called fool. They might not have known the names of things but understood the nomenclature for extreme reasons for crimes of passion or wanting what others had without working for it. They could categorize one's over exaggeration of one's self and knew the correct classification for thankless behavior. Their usage was drawn from Old Testament communication to capture impulses evoked during modern social interaction. While many of these descriptives are fast disappearing as elders die, behaviors they sought to define remain.

I am light on account of repercussions rising rhythmically from the skins of this language play, this randomly organized text. Simultaneously I am heavy inside. The very subject of mourning is kilogrammed. The fact that it concerns my Mother's transition is sufficient. These are self-evident. My Caribbean region's perception of disabilities now coursing through me continues to relay languages of concern. My Mother would be considered visually disabled, visually challenged, visually impaired, partial. St. Paul was partial: "now we see in part." Franklin Delano Roosevelt was known to have several disabilities. Visually challenged persons could be found all over from Harriet Tubman, to Galileo Galilei, Louis Braille to Ella Fitzgerald, Stevie Wonder to Ray Charles, Helen Keller, British MP David Blunkett to President of the Senate in Barbados Kerryann Ifill. Indeed, I thought a medical anthropologist needed to visit one of Dominica's eastern communities, where there are cases of choroidal blindness. A Canadian group of ophthalmologists visited finally, identifying a disorder they called "Laplaine dystrophy." Laplaine is the name of that eastern community. The old and middle-aged people with those blue/grey/ green eyes -- those people of that community whose genetics stretch back to Europe -- keep losing their sight. Clearly, a team of pure ophthalmologist would not be sufficient. Ophthalmology suggests its cause is irreversible -- not even God's breath knows. It marches on, blinding as it cuts a trail of disorder. Does it occur to ophthalmology that there is a sadness about sight-loss? Does it occur to those ophthalmologists costing their visits, that having something running in the body destined to cause a permanent disability irrespective of what is done or not done is terribly frightening? When such people are isolated or left to aloneness, they are already half defeated. Does this tell us about other dimensions of healing especially of the visually impaired? These people are community elders, raconteurs, might have been wonderful nurses, teachers, farmers, fishers whose subjectivities have matured. Will they ever be listened to? Is there a method, beyond those facilitated by measurement and quantifying instruments, for understanding how their thoughts and emotions are stringed as intraocular pressure changes? I know it takes time to accept, accommodate the visually challenged but, in the long run, eye disorders will not be cured without participation of the one carrying the disorder.

Moreover, visual impairment runs lines of taboo in many regions of the so-called developing world where as recently as 1990 in the US for example, significant laws have been passed to facilitate people, persons with disabilities. I come from a culture -- even in its media

-- which has only just begun to accept persons with disabilities. Once, like all communities across the world, they too made mockery of the blind the deaf, dumb and physically challenged. Those who do not speak we call them moumou. Clearly, this is changing as we move into the Twenty-First Century. At the end of the Twentieth, we were still largely at the level of the cripple deaf dumb and blind. The concepts impaired and physically or mentally challenged have -- like the words bling, bomb, hot and so on – just entered our everyday vocabulary. Has there been no Caribbean nation response to disability? Not at all. Jamaica has provided pedagogic instruments for persons willing to study disabilities in the Caribbean. Most of the graduates return to their island states to run meagerly financed institutions furnished with a limited even outdated bulk of assistive technology; our children living with autism are underserved and as in many developed countries, treated as nuisances and kept at home. Their cause is only now being recognized. Truly, they're trying to gene the damn thing, hiding the flaws of development paradigms.

In my country Dominica, the Association Of Persons With Disabilities has knowledge, but up to 2015, streets of the capital, business houses and performing centers were largely inaccessible – they were not built by those colonials with disabilities in mind. But you see, this new Millennium moves even the deadest of living things. Those regional disabilities associations have taken on cricket, blind cricket, forming teams, interestingly in an area of West Indian culture where our protagonists were no longer producing wins at World Cup competitions. When West Indian cricket begins to fail, West Indian pride is creaking. West Indian Blind move into position to salvage, not cricket in my view, but West Indian pride until some time when such skills can reap harvest of wins from sheer capacity and indeed, the spirit of dancing feet on pitches at Bourda, Kensington and Sabina. Let's see what the Caribbean Council for the Blind sees in this Third Millennium, moving as it should beyond mere treatment protocols. We need interpret floaters again, look into light and love rising on new horizons clearly visible to those visually impaired who're taught to recognize mystery behind their eyes. It's time!

In New York, social support is excellent. A man or woman carrying a cane is already innocent by law. When I visited the National Association for the Visually Handicapped in Manhattan I was told by its Executive Director, "you got to use the rest of your brain honey. Your brain can show you many things." The National Association for Visually Handicapped fired my passion.

NAVH described its mission as the restoration of self-esteem, independence and dignity to the visually impaired. Generally, in its literature, glaucoma does not figure as a disease that can be cured but one that the patient has to cope with. There is too, a voice, a single voice who encourages faith even as the records of vision reclamation thereby, remain bleakly negative. In fact, ophthalmologists I know would laugh at the idea of faith healing but it forms an integral part of modern alternative healing. Doctors of medicine are known to pray with their patients. I knew one optometrist who always reminded me that there is Hope. Whenever she said it, it sounded to me as if she knew of a medical breakthrough coming, or that alternative forms of healing such as energy medicine, were fast-emerging. She wasn't wrong. Generally however, schools have taught most eye specialists that glaucoma cannot be cured and can be treated only with eye drops and surgery. One ophthalmologist told me in New York, whenever I find a cure, he would be happy to know. Those students learn to repeat the incurable statement over and over again as the number of visits increase. Mama, eye-care paradigms are in crisis. Theories of seeing and seeing again do not provide space for finding cures. The Spirit of the Living God -- a magnificent field force -- haunts halls of ophthalmology and those who practice this gift are rushing into the rapture of technology to secure a semblance of efficiency. Their hearts pound as the nerve is revealed or a field-vision test casts a ball on a computer screen darkened half of it three quarters of it all of it. The eye is such wonderfully intricate anatomy that I believe people who seek to care for it should first experience losing part of it. Then the two hundred and fifty dollar visit will be more about mutual renewal than the legitimizing of self-interest.

It occurred to me also that the impersonal gaze extended way beyond the Caribbean. One Canadian ophthalmologist specializing in glaucoma had me as a patient for under a year and did not even know where I was from or which university I attended. He was very eager to look into the eyes to see the nature and extent of what they referred to as damage until I stopped his hand about to drop drops into my right eye. You know, they're human. They feel behind this distant profession. They get excited. I could feel their breath against my face as they looked at optic nerves. Ecstasy. Trust me. I've seen many of them. They observed my eyes, I observed their behavior. They had reason it seemed, to be excited. There is quite a catalogue of damaged sights in ophthalmology: those twisted right those closed those bulging not all from glaucoma off course. Imagine a Nineteenth Century eye collection bearing similarities with a late Twentieth Century collection much like a history of photography cataloguing the sensual ragged rugged delightful wild dangerous hungry deep wicked kind evil sardonic bright sad hazel radiant defiant black. They titillate ophthalmologists. It's amazing what the eyes can become when observed. It's amazing, their potential as media.

My Father who enjoyed the company, knowledge, mystic sayings and rituals of priests was drawn to obstetrics/ gynecology as much as he might have to the Jesuits. He remembered in the early days of training for the priesthood the young student was supposed to lift a tea-cup by focusing on it. The eyes power-secrets may still be alive in the Russian Orthodox Church!

CHAPTER 25

Eye Treatment Business

In Mama's youth days on island there were no medical insurance companies. Government paid doctors to visit local clinics and those called dispensers to read and interpret. When I was a child in the sixties that was still the case. By the early 1980s, she was paying for private visits in the city. That was however optometric. Dominica received its first foreign ophthalmologist in 1985, and in 1996 a national took on the task of ophthalmology.

Though at the beginning of this millennium, a 2001 Housing and Population Census placed the number of persons with sight disability at 773 out of a 70,000 population, the figure remains debatable. In 2008, the island's sole ophthalmologist was reporting 420 cases, 50% of which could be attributed to cataract and 20% to glaucoma. But persons working in the field report higher figures. Truly, at this stage, one more is too many.

Though an intelligent woman in accounting and time-keeping, our Mother and many like her in the early 80s, did not question the optometrist and ophthalmologist. They followed prescriptions to the letter. They were however informed significantly subjectively, since they carried the disorder as phenomenon, experiencing its fog and clarity, its pain and frustrations personally. Clinical methods did not entail subjectivities and feelings -- medical schools were thus designed whether in the colonies, North America or Europe. Doctor was the keeper of objective, empirical knowledge and thus power. In the islands, while patients did not ask a question of the physician, he -- it was a "he" one hundred percent of the times -- impressed on them that as long as they followed the prescription everything would be alright. Coming from a tradition of popular herbal medicine, they were accustomed to follow through and be consistent, and that, more as a natural delight rather than a perceived inconvenience to be included in their everyday life. Everything would be alright meant the physiological problem would be solved, the disorder ordered, the disease eased. People then were healthier; let us not forget quality of food was primarily organic, naturally grown, most times prepared, consumed at home, among family immediate or extended. In many cases just the fact that they eat together or saw the doctor made them well. The doctor was the knowledge store often times from a different class. Poor people's children did not get the opportunity to do medicine until the late 1970s and early 80s when Havana and my Marxist dialectics book donors cared enough to help. Doctor was dressed smartly differently, used instruments not normally available to the lay and had attended school overseas. Doctor was supposed to know how to fix the problem. It was an accepted belief, one propagated and subsequently instilled or one which, by way of an ideological process conditioned people to conform to doctors diagnoses over and above their indigenous herbal knowledge and inherited practices. In fact except in the case of topical applications to sores and other abrasions which entailed healing time, many internal matters were usually eased simply by the doctor's word. Off course his word would not dislodge a tape-worm! I am reminded that prescribed medicine then was of a better quality; the distinction between generic and brand name was not yet democratized.

While suggesting that there were and are women and men of exceptional intuitive and diagnostic skill in the profession today, it is also clear today that the science's methods will not be salvaged by state-of-the-art technology. MRI allows us to see. We must then cure. Science is the search for Truth and Truth can no longer be restricted in a caring art to exercises in treatment trials. Crisis? In the case of ophthalmology, the eye may be the last place to look! As for alternative medicine, mainstream eye doctors advise patients against its use. Though the smoking of cannabis lowers intraocular pressure, it also lowers blood pressure one mainstreamer argued. Today, they scramble to medicalize it -- echoes of Jamaican singer Peter Tosh ring out inside Europe's parliaments, across the Americas and Caribbean Community! Cannabis can be steamed, drawn and used to flavor sauces. Some dare to make marijuana cookies or cakes, but the expert warns: brownies are particularly dangerous. Another was concerned about the quantity that had to be ingested over time and the subsequent diminishing returns in effect. Today, the THC is extracted and placed in pessaries and patches for administering to HIV-AIDS and cancer patients. Among other benefits, it stimulates their appetite. Peter Tosh, one of reggae's most outspoken advocates told governments of the world, if they legalized it, he would "advertise it!" It was, he contended the "only cure for glaucoma." Not only does it lower intraocular pressure, adds one Ethiopian-based Dominican herbalist, it impacts on the hypothalamus. I knew one Dominican gentleman whose eye was badly hurt and cut by a cricket ball while playing in a friendly match at UWI, Mona Jamaica. Not only did he come to see completely again, the eye body with its delicate tissue, was regenerated after his marijuana treatments. He may have been a special case, but I like the fact that his eye was cured, made whole again!

In New York, one Beth Israel ophthalmologist was of the view that herbal medicine sometimes caused more harm than good to the human body. Still a herbalist was convinced that disorders such as Glaucoma were caused by a build-up of mucus around the affected organ or in the body in general. Still another thought the optic nerve was not damaged, but smothered in mucus. An ophthalmologist showed me how the optic nerves were like a broken anchor, the chain having no ground in its swing from left to right. Scary at the front of the face! That view of the structure of the optic nerve and its path is indeed wrong. A quantum healer told me that Glaucoma is caused by congestion in the body. I can subscribe to the finding that glaucoma involves degeneration of retinal ganglion cells. That should be able to be replenished however. Here is the opportunity in crisis: ophthalmologists need to work with plant-based nutritionists. One is forced to ask, do ophthalmologists ever even consider nutritionists? The human eye is so responsive, calling for the drops when those are forgotten. They show their addiction to small amounts of cocaine in eye drops. Just think of the benefits of excellent nutrition on the gentle tissue of the eye body and its vascular spread. We walk with pharmaceutical side effects like dancers, knowing them to be our silent partners for life, dwelling in a private and latinized sanctuary named the human body. Just imagine nutrition for the genes or optic nerve or brain!. In 2015, they call forth, at last, a combination of possibilities named gene therapy. Just imagine nutrition's long-term journey through cells in that body lighting up their membranes. The language of its parts is as complex as the accounting practices of multinational corporations. And yet beyond those streets the labyrinthine spread of ganglia, channels, passages, islets and chambers, irises, nuclei, magnetic fields and warm blood in heat fed by Fire -- this body is a beautiful and indeed awesome creation! To know its structure and function is to be intimate with it and Word's mystery.

I hear a choir of children in my youth singing "there is power / power / wonder-working power / in the blood of the Lamb." I even hear the echoes -- a quality of angelic strains, the kind associated with hosts in a sort of ascendancy. Heard where the power was? In the blood of the Lamb. They didn't sing "a Lamb." Then it could be anyone. Mary had a little Lamb its fleece was white as snow. Most of our Lambs were brown and we seldom saw the blood; when one was slaughtered that was the end of the blood. What was the difference in the blood of a chicken bull goat porpoise pig and lamb. Those boyhood days?

First to begin, we called all -- lamb and ram -- sheep. Furthermore, we did not understand the difference between the sacrifice of an animal and that of a human being. As a practice, our people did not sacrifice humans, neither did human beings in our time speak of sacrificing through their blood. They would sacrifice a bit of time to help a neighbor during koudmein, but never through their death or open shedding of blood. What was the difference in the blood power -- that between Jesus Christ' blood and any other blood sacrifice? And throughout Jesus' time, what did blood come to mean as medium. Was there blood more precious than other bloods? What was a sacrifice? Was the sacrificed body like the oceans which could absorb all bodies like rivers? Was there a universal eye, an eye seeing everywhere? Children might have asked those in order to connect with Jesus who did so many miraculous things. Children thought Jesus was quiet and well-behaved -- we wanted to be like Jesus. But if we did not play we became dull and sleepy. If we did not dance we were usually ones left out of the party. If a boy could not swim he could not go to the basèn or out to sea -- Jesus and his disciples could swim. Then there were those who had an attack of measles or chicken pox and wondered about the power in the blood. Truth is, innocence did not know how to connect: we only had to believe that the spirit of a man who lived two thousand years ago moves, lives in us still. Powerful, is it not? For what it says, at least, this is potential. How old therefore is flesh? How does it communicate. Aren't its thought-waves visible electromagnetically? Does knowing Christ teach us more about science than science itself will ever imagine? Do science and spirituality really need a rendezvous? Truth and beauty are well-known lovers in the Heavens and on Earth, through alleys of stars, down oceans depths, from an eagle's flight to an infant's hold. Behold beauty in that which remains when all flesh is stripped. Behold an ultimate truth. Bones of the face keep sockets in place. As for the skull -- with two bones in an X shape under -- it remains a sign marking a dangerous place, a poison. Such a permanently strong structure, so full of beauty and truth holding the spinal length with integrity -- such is used to construct a sign of a killing substance. Along its stretch, chakras emanate energy as was meant to be their duty, function. Under the skull sits the brain -- the greatest pharmacy. Bones forming the chin know those of the cheek -- tissue under the eye is so tender to an acupuncturist's needle. Then there's the forehead behind which so much moves, is in motion from the pituitary to the pineal and then the candle in the open roof, the crown -- its light shooting out as if the top middle of the head had a window reaching to the outside with its light, its sound, its waves, its heat that the blind spot locks into. Something, somebody chose to structure on a foundation of bones, none of which were broken in the body of Christ Jesus. It was noted.

You know, we sang about blood, heart, mind, dreams, visions, rivers, seas, light, feet, you know -- I never heard us sing there is power, power in the bone. We just sang and like most other things we did in those days we did not think of thinking. The marrow should have been activated automatically. In fact it should have known we were going to sing about it that morning. Blood records and knows past present and future as if they are before it in one shape and time. We should've sung: there is power, wonderworking knowledge in the blood of the lamb. Knowledge in the blood of a lamb or the lamb? Whichever. Our bodies, though corruptible were still largely uncontaminated, interconnected with our eco, electrified, emanating pure energy, truly in a mode of play and joyful perception. Thing is -- and to many, this should not be factored -- despite our claim to childlike purity, historic strains of denying the body's inherent power had crossed over into our inheritance, our promised property, blurring our perception of the kingdom, the paradise, the liquid energy, the spiritual abode, the gifts in, within us. In the language of pure war, we have to wipe out these strains. It has to be a flawless assault from roots of gentlest tissue and unblended cell chemistry too!

CHAPTER 26

Blinking Resurrection Fire

Along the path of this narrative I became increasingly conscious of the spiritual power in this inevitability, this passing this dying. In fact I realized that Christ's recorded triumph over death will remain a story an event of everlasting might. Save for The Lazarus Phenomenon which Jesus Christ performed, the raising of Christ Jesus himself from the dead is an awesome stunner downplayed by the scientific. This resurrection is height of rebel force ultimate victory shouting: take the flesh take the blood and even as you take them I have already given mine to those who believe. As an aside, stem cell research hopes to restore dead cells. What is amazingly revealing for practitioners of Ayurveda is that the stem cells can be drawn from the patient's body as much as it can be from embryos. While the embryo as source remains a debate among military moralists the idea of finding stems cells for optic nerve growth in the nasal passage of the patient answers in part to the issue of all things being in the human -- the old maxim that the body when left to itself can heal. Since the entire project is so tainted with distrust, lines cannot be drawn. Man in this case, is such an ambitious creature. Though embroiled in controversy, the stem cell matter points to a coming hope an answer partial, yes, but evidence of the greater more complete setting free. Imagine men women technologists, scientists talking about treating preventing and curing!

The idea must have arisen out of the Earth one evening while walking, the soles against the land and precious thoughts crossing unconsciously, involuntarily up time's body, its ancient heel. Be still. This old soul is returning now, coming back through the soles of women and men who care to make greeting the Earth a daily practice. It returns now in the eyes of alert new-borns. This is the body the one that triumphs over death. It is the body that will restore your sick and troubled. It is the body that endures long -- the fittest. This is the body that will be fed. This is the mind that conceives and achieves. This is thought following rivers paths, the eagle the sisserou. This is the blood that has to be cared. The older ones -- your founding Mothers and Fathers -- use to purify it with bitter bushes and herbs to ward off those suckers. This? This is the blood that flows to the brain feeding the occipital frontal and temporal lobes. This is the blood in the hand that shakes congratulations out of truth and sincerity. This is the hand that heals. This is the subconsciousness that chooses to stand for justice. Let not your heart be troubled by disease, attacks, strokes. He did not say it, this does not mean we should not understand it thus.

I remember almost twenty years ago a broadcaster colleague told me her heart was for pumping blood. She did not see this Love function in motion in warmth in heat in Fire. I understand her influences. Remember Tina Turner's 1985 smash-hit "What's Love Got To Do With It?" Recall that major question: "who needs a heart when a heart" -- like china – "can be broken?" She subscribed to a medical model; she, like Tina must have been a cardiologist in her former Life. I wondered whether in her world, there was a clear connection between rush of blood and feelings of warmth anger love -- my heart used to beat faster when I saw my girlfriend. This, my broadcaster friend would argue is not about love but an ancient precursor to sexuality. I may have to find out from her since she became a Mother and by way of a man. Was he animal in expression? Or was conception surrogated? She never felt that rush of his coming at her moistened gate? She never had time to think? It is just that she did not connect spirit of the Ancient of Days with sex and heart. A Christian wife is quite passionate to her husband, even more so as a girlfriend, her ecstasy dripping wet behind a fiery commandment. Fire in and of hearts? St. Paul however rages against sexual immorality and, warns not to give Satan any opportunity to enter between the bodies of husband and wife. Their hearts like their bodies should pulsate ideally as one. He, St. Paul describes our God as a consuming Fire! Woooo. At the core of the heart's primitive cells? Woooo. Smelt me, melt me, purify me, restore, reconstruct me, glaze me here and now Jah, now that I may find victory in this Life and the one to come, the many, many to come. Open your eyes! Blink! A thousand ages. Blink, consuming Fire, just blink. Bring healing. Cure Blinking Resurrection Fire. Cure. As you advance, recover. We can no longer believe. It's time to know. We don't have the money to purchase those miracle eye-cures. We don't have coverage means. We cannot pay COPAY. So pour something else on us. Pour some hypothalamic light into our pituitary. Mingle our sebum. Let your anointing, your new creature chemistry rise in us. Let our hearts law beat in a way that draws our attention to this novel, exciting rhythm coming at us.

Tell you why spirit's justice marching into crisis fills me with joy? Historically, for me as a Caribbean person the body was a source of labor and experimentation. Torture was rife. Levels of resistance to pain was well measured. Men and women were pushed to maximum bodily endurance under weight of punishment by whip machete gunshot ripping of entrails branding cutting of external protruding members imprisonment rape of women and children repressed in religion and evil. The body as architecture was supposed to be denied, rejected as sinful devilish guilt-ridden full of curses and in the case of our men too potent. Too many of our women were raped by law. Carnal knowledge was lawful. The body was to be a desert, a place hated by those who came from desert winds, who knew their forests before thieves came to civilize. That's not all. A body enslaved was being told by select preachers that someone, that special someone who died once for all, that someone at a table where wine and bread were being served centuries ago, told his followers: this is my body given for you. That body resurrected.

This should no longer be a captive body. Agreed, right? However, true economy of light was hindered by dark intentions rooted in supremacy. My people persisted: saved once for all by the Lord Jesus Christ, yet enslaved. Who could have survived this schizophrenia, save those who knew Christ's message to the world before Europe became dark, before Las Casas preached, before Columbus sailed. Today we celebrate the body not only because its memories remember those we never met. They inform our silences. They speak to our fears of dying. They relay the outcome of our endurance to heights and depths of our minds and Spirit -- thoughts are precious in this place. It is not out of a desire to mock that we return. It is not even to settle a score with our captors and oppressors. There are just places justice has to reach.

CHAPTER 27

Not Rocket Art Nor Science

Spiritual healing is borderless impacting on a pattern of emotions as it courses the oceans of the body, its shimmering waterways, its exquisite endocrinology, its glands, pounds of cartilage, its defenses its mitochondria's fires. Thoughts take to racing on highways of mind even as birds take to the sky or dogs bark before the hurricane or tremor. Ready? The body is about to receive its first-time guest -- an unaccustomed yet known visitor. The critical history of that visitor indicates déjà, mission accomplished -- dread silence to and within an ancient body. There's this too: joy, the rejoicing, giving thanks in song and prayer embraces and blessings. It is sisters, brothers dwelling together in unity anointing. Thoughts are catapulted. They must effect changes in flesh and blood chemistry: the face shines. That which is curled up is shifted, made straight. Dead cells are covered with living ones and disappear. Atrophied muscles brought to life shimmer in rain. Joints find their cartilage, sinews their threads and Electricity -- horizontally bed-ridden bodies are lifted. Energies locked in the solar plexus awake chakras covered by mucus, open the ears to sound and loose the tongue. "Like the Ocean is your God-self," Kahlil Gibran noted, "it is forever undefiled." Not only is this a compelling ecological suggestion. It speaks to nature's capacity for repair. The whole retains a quantum essence. It is like saying by God's unmerited favor we are restored.

I never forget what a Rabbi told me. In Jewish cosmology, he said, God sometimes becomes divorced from himself. There is a whole greater than itself and the sum of its parts constituted in the negation of its wholeness. There is a power greater than disease, death. Heia there is a power greater than Life itself. St. Paul contends that that power greater than life and death is in the love of God which is in Christ Jesus. He is convinced beyond death that nothing in life, nothing in death, not angels not principalities or powers or things present or things to come, nothing in the heights or depths can ever again separate us from the love of God which is in Jesus Christ. Mama loved that. Blindness, no matter how dreadful, could not separate her from that Love. I believe its light chemistry, its liquid energy simply needed to percolate into actual seeing. It's not rocket art nor science. This love represents part of NASA's hopes for its astronauts killed on entry into Earth's atmosphere. It encompasses feelings of grief expressed by families of the 9/11 dead. It covers the 27,000 tortured during Pinochet's rule in Chile; the 40,000 mine-victims in Angola; those slaughtered by Idi Amin and Milosevic; those whose lands and houses have been helplessly consumed in volcanic ash, sucked by a yawning earth or tossed in the floods of a hurricane. Millions of birds cannot sing from the thick of Lebanon's oil spills, neither can the hundreds bombed in its market places, but this Love covers their silencing. Death cannot separate us. This is profound promise, an assurance, Mama used to say, that passeth all understanding. This is super-abundant. It almost says that all are invited to feast. This great invitation sent faster than instant, was designed, packaged by Christ more than two thousand years ago. What happened from year one to one thousand to upset this gift of love which actually worked in the body!

No illusion. Take courage. There is another generation of Gospel interpreters coming to turn the stones of what I care to call religious economics. A Caribbean historical experience is living testimony to this movement against all odds. It is a journey through the accounting sheets of merchant capital, raw testing of flesh and blood by industrial torture, the course of production deadlines rising steep unflinching in its cruel demands. My Mother's grandparents encountered strange men strange in their engagements with evil forces by way of Latin incantations cryptic utterances and blood sacrifices. They met ships clergy, abolitionists apprentices. We crossed through passages by way of crown colonies associated states violence law schisms of lords and serfs kings and queens popes and tyrants presidents and prime ministers. Something has to be with this people who burn at a tree or break humans at a treadmill and continue to praise a Lord. These people had to be evil mad. It is an ancient story!

CHAPTER 28

That Wonderfilled Resilience

Dominica's Reverend William Watty in an Easter sermon delivered at the Bethesda Methodist Church in Dominica's capital, noted that with the rolling away of the stone from the tomb which held the body of Jesus Christ and with his resurrection, The problem is there but it is no longer a problem. It is now an antique! True it has a history of stratification harking back to another time when humanity might have been more auditory than visual. For all we know, its granite might have been more visible to the naked eye. It is still there but now as part of the landscape. It is still there but no longer a barrier. This is a powerful and spirit-filled psychological moment. Pause a while and think of the implications for healing miracles and cures. It's all about how we think about it. This is a generation's challenge: switching to another plane leaving flesh and blood to its process. Did anyone say no medicine? No. We entertain psychological progeny, ancestral connects, anointings, players from timelessness, spirit-filled counsels, excellent diagnosticians, gifted surgeons, silences. We have to know, not just believe. We have to know the place, visit and enter at will, find at will to heal, heal, find a medicine wheel to respond to our urgencies, community to the bone, communion to the core, communication to the salted letter.

Tell you, it's a time abundant when they of that generation encounter the problem, but it no longer exists in their thinking. They've overcome. But there is one supreme problem: death. The pastor argues however that Jesus Christ has advanced beyond that, beyond life's supreme problem: death. Every barrier has been removed; every wall breached every blind eye now becomes a highway. A highway? Who, what travels thereby? Who is the seer, how do we see now that death is swallowed up? Does my sight condition change in the physical while I am alive? Does this psychological attitude overcome the gene thing?

Or, is the gene thing so strong, that irrespective of who runs the highway, they will allow for no distance viewing beyond a hands length? Is thought shifting cell environments? Long night's discourse, is it not? Death is still there, but it is no longer a problem. Death was swallowed up. You would've thought after the death and resurrection of Christ Jesus, death would be no more. You would've thought that following the resurrection of Christ Jesus no one under the Sun would die after this day on Golgotha. You would've thought. Did we miss something as this Love paradigm rolled through town? Death no more? A seed knows better, dying to burst forth.

Truly, a burgeoning religious history of Caribbean lands strives to position Christ Jesus as victorious not only over enslavement oppression and all forms of captivity, but over disease and death. Christ Jesus is therein, sustainability, liberation, -- the kind that brings joy and strength from whence it started to now; from now to where generations can praise those who defended their rights to clean water at the very least. To too many of my people Jesus Christ was at the center of their will to plant provision grounds within plantation society's mono-crop. This wonderful resilience? Hear this. Dasheen sweet potatoes cush-cush yams tannias cassava plantains bananas when well prepared surpass macaroni and cheese and rice. They gave us the raw.

My friend Mallika Samuel who holds a fine knowledge of the work of female Rastafarians/Dreads in Dominica in the 70s told me those people of the late 19th. and early 20th. Centuries, also planted hopes fruit trees herbs for both food and medicine. They cultivated barks and flowers available to this day. Death or threats of death punishment legal action or imprisonment did not stop the herbal, the nutritious pass over. To mark, brand for sale, cut off an ear, use the body as a page on which an invisible letter is written and the only sign is one consummated in miscegenation, hybridization, to mark it, to label as folk devil, does not stop this borderless march, this "realeyesing" of a spiritual awakening itself an echo of a universal movement keeping its promise that those who know it shall recognize its ray-stretching entry into human motion, behind human eyes, into human bone. Listen.

The matter which captures my attention is the unexpected occurrence. The slip and fall and fracture, a swinging door that slams the elbow, the centipede that finds you and you alone to sting, the man knocked down by a vehicle on a road he has traveled for years, the woman who suddenly loses her child, the knife that cuts, the tongue that is bitten, the first string bursting in the middle of a favorite song, the bridge suddenly falling, a slip in the bathroom, the accident happening to friends who were with you two minutes before the sudden change in feeling into sickness, the decision to release oneself to a captor to death to suicide to forgiving, the thought that changes your life forever that day you said yes or no or spoke and wish you hadn't, that day you remained silent. You know those moments when you took the bowl of rice and one grain "stick" and the coughing began. You remember the bone sticking in your throat was from the juiciest piece of fish. I've walked from where I live just five yards to the main road and step straight into a sting. You remember the night you had sex and pelvic inflammatory pain the morning after. Those inexplicables? Mama used to say, let Thy will be done! I believe we have to understand these moments and minimize their negative impact on our lives. We, people of African descent in the Caribbean must know that Christ has given us consciousness. Is our consciousness embracing its subconsciousness?

The writer sits at her processor cancer in her breast. Makes me angry. She's older than me yet I can see her transforming sadness into idea into hope into enlightenment. She fights within the pain over the pain with the pain churning magnificence. I guess it does not matter when the cells began their secret pathogenic intercourse heralding death. What if there was no suffering. Would the works have been just as poignant in fire when pain cries for recognition and you in that glorious flight hold with clan power in vengeance to the letter. We even justify paying dues. We say if we did not suffer if we were not punished we would not have risen to such heights.

I feel narrow walking this road of freedoms: freedom from fear suppression suffering. My thoughts are probably being influenced now by a television documentary on childbirth and the use of a spinal anesthesia, an epidural. For years despite the obvious I mused over my Father's saying: nobody likes pain. I am forever looking into the text of his speech beyond his words which, though spoken in English, were rooted in a French lexicon. They could also be English and that alone. NO body likes pain is a perfect sentence. With license granted me as owner of his property I can say he coded the text to mean a body likes pleasure. There is no doubt that every body likes pleasure. Think of the pleasure of touch or the curl of a mammals body as it sucks from its Mother. Elders in Japan were said to find pleasure by touching a furry-soft outer coating designed for robots. Mama, I'm tripping. Kissing picturesque ideas? Sucking cray in a good meal's delights. Pleasure. There are sites in nature that bring tears to human(ize). Songs can bring joy to tears.

You know, on a lighter side of heavy, our country dinners were more about Shakespeare, Voltaire, Rousseau, Hugo, Huxley, Claudel and Au Coeur De Troisieme Reich and, exercising power in human thought. Lighter side of heavy? We were less about pain and more about pleasures in philosophy. As for comments on death, I recall my Father saying the dead can do you nothing. It is the living, reality, everyday life, the world's reality that kills. To many, reality is the bill the mortgage the children's education retirement sickness disease death. Between these words are biographies of distance and pain joy and strength anonymity and victory. The majority of mankind needs know another reality, other than pain suffering and death. The majority of human beings do not want to fight wars. The majority of human beings want to be disease free to live and see their children live to see them swim in rivers and seas drink clean water eat healthy food and learn truth whether in Mathematics Biology or History of Art. So many grandparents from all cultures love to see their children's children sing, run strong, dance, answer to a question, solve a problem speak clearly, act intelligently. My God! So many people around the world are content to do a day's work return to their homes and praise their totem poles. They do not want bombs falling on their houses or blood running from their children's noses along Cruel paths of broken bones shattered limbs and smashed-in faces. What trauma? Every child should be taught rudiments of pain resistance. There is a chemistry in the human brain which like psychiatry has much to teach humanity. Nobody likes pain. I came that you might have life and have it abundantly at the micro and macro levels. Abundance implies total coverage, even protection when crossing busy streets. Just imagine whispering a prayer while placing the hand on the forehead in times of a headache, and the pain vanishing? What is it that would've flowed into your hands when you said Christ, or simply touched with compassionate belief? What is the age of that current? But you know, there is a pain that rewards, that does not kill. It is evident in the athlete overcoming, the dancer's exceptional memory. It is effervescence when they overcome pain in bodies tautly tensed muscles, gain mastery, win any battle thrill spectators and audiences. Learning to play the guitar was painful but as the weeks progress the pain gives way to strength and delight. Long hard hours steel the construction worker to a threshold of pleasure in muscle lifting, to the point where the arm misses the exercise. The hand holding a brush finds that over time the brush moves with ease as if the hand moving it was another inside the one holding it. It's painful being a carpenter's apprentice, but over time the saw becomes light.

Does disease cause us therefore to rise above our selves. Does the vain suffer more than the selfless or the captain less than his human cargo? When a woman flies from the deck of a slave-ship child in arms where is pain in this act of courage. And what of those who grieve knowing freedom day is nigh, yet die daily as they see their young walk out each day to fields of terror. What is the nature of the pain of those who never suffer any physical fracture injury or strain and die in silence in the hours when nature is the darkest and all else is asleep. There is more to the human brain than the analytic and logical.

Mama, "bless the Lord O my soul and all that is within me bless his holy name," is a veritable trumpet call to education. In light of the promise of victory over death as subject this is a liberation text restoring, reclaiming territory parcel by parcel bit by bit joint by joint sinew by sinew cell by cell drop by drop.

CHAPTER 29

We Never Moved Alone

This narrative is not only for "natives of my person," but for those raped and castrated by a hybridized patriarchy. It is too for those whose lights went out picking cotton whose lands were stolen, burial-grounds desecrated, identity surgically scarred by those whose angst boils whose racism becomes a pale prison whose lands are ripped by machines greed and chemical waste whose livelihoods are destroyed by others and their own, whose people disappear with no report. We say from behind our inherited song, between our palm and sculpting knife, from the middle of our harvest no matter what they say about our poverty, we say that to treat the part thoroughly, by any means, we must embrace the whole. It is intelligence that puts faith to work, that engages me and not only me but an entire region that knows faith to work in individual economics but seldom in matters of cure. It is to create a condition of independence from a medical profession in transition and crisis that I struggle. Say what you want call me what you bleed! The people of those West Indies have a specific historical experience revealing power of the living God in ways too troubling to the dogmatic, the atheistic. In our tradition, which incidentally has been made confusing by the historic and theologic arrivants, our Mothers say that as Alpha and Omega Christ holds the key to the transformation of mind and spirit. Yet that spirit needs cross into and impact on body. Does that mean it does not happen. No not at all. It has to become a studied act executed with the power of all that is within. The within moves but there are invisible chains in mind. To use maybe partially a Freudian analogy the id is alive. The ego vibrates. The superego bridges the two functions but as though smothered. It operates like a checkpoint controlled by a vicious military with instruments of fear for purposes of torture. In that world Satan is Black. I speak as one born in the Caribbean where religion, which is supposed to connect even after its affirmation of resurrection, is still the stumbling block, stone at the mouth of a tomb. Fortunately, wise liberation pastors, like our song-poets, composers, musicians and artists have consistently kept us ahead of the game -- essentially in the loop of consciousness. Steel Pulse, Reggae intelligences of the dawn of the Twenty-First Century call for all invisible chains to be broken -- visible ones cannot return. They will be melted on arrival. Religion, they contend, has been the "backbone of our strife." Imagine how this spinal functions and to what end. Those Reggae masters conclude that false prophets have "misguided our lives."

In the history of the Caribbean, Rastafarians like members of the Steel Pulse band, are the only movement I know to give the "I" a place beyond the selfish centered. The "I" in their world-view lived beyond Freud's individual unconscious, Freud's id. It represented a spiritually maturing entity, a liberation medium. Through its stages of development, the "I" transcends the material world but that world is not excluded from a collective vision. In fact it takes the spiritual matter and brings it to bear on the material the visible the temporal. It invests the physio(logical) and (an(atomic with transcendent energy. The first person becomes in their world a precious and simultaneously destructive utterance -- a magnification, if not a reflection of the larger person over and beyond one's own thinking, one's surrender. We're moving in the positive. "I" is timely response, the self opening to the will of Creator's creative energies and powers of discernment. The "I" represents an inner force trickling, that when allowed speaks the positive, that when granted, supports frail negative spirits infusing them with refreshing, restorative sayings, active knowledge, lucid rewards. Strong negatives might well have been read as meditation time communication time, sifting hour. Somebody's knocking. Inspiration gifts work faster than bodies can cycle, Recycle. Those millions of neurons will not wait for you to adjust when chemical tides come flooding. You just got to move! One song-writer helped us along that way, when he sang, "move and groove." The moving "I" encapsulates seeds of ancestral wisdom, secrets of healing, ways of knowing that even Guyanese historian Walter Rodney cited. Individuals finding joy in such relations love Sun Moon and Stars rivers and oceans plants and herbs salt and fresh-water life Wind fresh Air Fire and its transforming powers, soil birds night and dawn's early light to cite song-writer David Rudder and the US anthem, the rainbow's violet indigo blue green yellow orange red, healthy foods colorful meaningful comfortable clothing uplifting language music speaking to sense of joy Oneness and hopeful promises in their convocation to meet. Wow! They are known to love the communicative, networking capability of ants. Those men and women awakening in a pre-independence Caribbean were not alone under their lock of nappy. They formed part of, and influenced movements worldwide cutting an inspiring cultural path antithetical to governments and yet seminal to the political integrity of peoples universally. Calls for a holistic life living with heart mind and soul could never be explained away as additional deviant variables. They could not be explained away as a series of evolving negations. This was a tremendous effort at connecting a people, yet one that could not commit the error of leaving them in a desensitized, comatose, aphasic condition.

Effervescent, budding youth movements should know that all was not well in the Rastafarian camp. Not only did political and legal systems shoot their bodies. They too had to be reminded by Bunny Wailer years later that "Rasta don't fire 'pon Rasta." Importantly however, in their world-view, we the children of African slaves, Asian migrants and European off-shoots had witnessed ravages of a brutal enemy. An enemy had waged war against African people and their descendants, wiped out native people of the Americas and the Caribbean, slandered Selassie, sold Garvey shot Gandhi and King imprisoned Mandela, murdered Biko and Malcolm, crucified Jesus Christ and so many others.

Christ, as we know him is every person's right to be. This is walking in humility time. Flesh will not contain the spirit of the living God. That spirit moves. Flesh has to contend with its external manifestation its bowl its Water and Air food and sleep rest and work. Out of its mouth comes sound which is as invisible as Wind. In a culture of death people kill such wonderful forms. Healing must take the place of killing.

CHAPTER 30

Water and Justice May Be Served

The body "who" dies, the body buried gives back to Earth all that Earth gave to it. From in utero stages where Mother serves as medium through his or her lifetime and passing, that body is sustained by Earth's resources. We must teach this more directly. It's clear today, that application of spiritual energy to everyday life, to just economic activity, to improved human relations and respect for Earth Mother, remain the single most important challenge to any sort of religious or spiritual practice. While it is true that one may acquire riches and be philanthropic benevolent and humanitarian, applying one's wealth to the satisfaction of human needs remains a rich blessing. Yes, Life seems futile at times, but a simple good deed each day returns.

We are connected. We live in cycles. A farmer using leaves from an uprooted tuber to create a compost heap is demonstrating awareness of nature's oneness yet may not be aware that that same relation (ship) travels with his human body. Cycles of return?

From the poetic eye of a dis-ease I shout: the body returns in the hurricane, Air filling the drum, breath of a pan-man cry of a baby just born in balmy morning temperatures. I could invest her breath in lit firewood in a main-sail's curve or a boom's rattle in the prophet's song between a finger and a trigger against a running child between her feet and the ground between her fall and the dust in her Mother's arms warm like blood in anger. Blood makes a difference. What about water stream? Brings to mind anthropologist Melville Herskovits footnoting that in Haitian culture There was a belief in a Water world in which the dead sojourns until those who are left to mourn do something good to redeem its spirit. It had to be a human gesture of mutual support to the divine will to purify to wash away sin. It suggests a return to innocence, an original innocence, a re-baptism. It also electrifies flow of life, unblocks rivers made dead by errors in a deforested conscience. It appears to me that in their world-view we are always being born. To do so in Christ, the Bible states, is to become a new creature. Lord, I gave all I had to the poor and followed every law from my youth to this day. You must be born again to enter the Kingdom of Heaven. Mama! Using a taken-for-granted element such as water by way of libations, the Haitian becomes a partner in the process. It may not find a place in orthodoxy's water ritual, but it is done.

Though much of the body is comprised of water, does this outpouring ensure being born again? Maybe by just being in the sun, feeling heat in its hydrogen and oxygen, we're lifted. Transformation in heart is key, a wise teacher suggests. It is the source of blood's communication. There must be a source to water that is not easily, readily reached inside the body, eh stream? It can wet our tongues at times. At times we can taste purity from within, a cleansing effect combined, or freely issuing as it does with a renewed state of mind and heart. It comes with physical fitness and health too. It comes after being slain in the spirit. It is in a baby's dribble. It is consummated in and through the Christ figure -- a representation not only of the much promulgated peace but indeed, one of justice. Just ice? Justice is not cold, frozen. Justice is compassion stirring brain's poised chemistry, its vibrant pharmacy.

Listen. People are hungry, having traveled long. They're emotionally strained. Among them, the poor sought renewal and blessings derived from true abundance. They might have been tired of double standards, rulers living in plenty claiming to cling to the law of Moses even as they coveted, stole paying wages sufficient for the return of the exploited. Jesus fed them from fields, hands plucking grain to the grinding through stone and Fire a weaved towel and basket handed by hands which prepared them, not knowing that moment to be the will of One named I Am. This here, represents beginning of the conjugation of the verb to be. He fed them from ocean depth, from life in salt by way of fishermen and boats nets muscle memory and instinct protein in bone. He fed them first. They had the larger feast consummated in a miracle lifting fire in their stomachs. But justice is more than just a human need for food. What about the Word sinking into soul's fire, cutting between joint and marrow? So many international institutions jump straight to peace thinking that food alone brings peace. Hey, propagating satisfying hunger is ideological business, military politics. The justice discourse offends the political directorate who depend on churches to quell that riot the Word inspires, instigates. True, a malnourished body barely has interest in acquiring knowledge. Peace is not a mechanical phenomenon. Peace is not a military achievement. My peace I leave with you was uttered after the just victory over death and a culture of hunger, poverty and violence.

Justice has to be done. The body had to be restored. In fact, the spirit soars over beyond chains of death, prisons of repression, haunt of manufactured fears, details in sadness over loss terror and helplessness in the face of futility disease daily discomfort rising to horrors of pain under hours and the Sun, nailed by loneliness childlessness, blindness. There is a sadness about life today. Yet for so many, it is the end of the road that tips the fervid scales. It is just at the touching point when they're about to give in that an answer shines, a door cracks open. Justice may be served when the poor go down never having realized a dream. Justice may be served when the weak give in and descend into days of apathy after apathy. Justice may be served in those ways. I do not agree but the scales of time have their own appropriate measure and death in one may reveal life in another. Justice knows that there is naivete in the goodness of the heart. Though justice stands by the poor, justice knows the poor can be wicked too. They too are angry. So many are melted within, bitter and ashamed, dangerous when doing things learnt from the rich. Justice too, finds good hearts among the rich, but on a large scale the world's rich nations are anxious about the present path of time. It points to an unprecedented engagement, appointment with justice. Justice lyrics? "Everybody wants to go up to Heaven," sings Jamaican Peter Tosh, "but nobody/nobody wants to die." He was calling for equal rights and justice!

A culture of death envisions peace in Heaven only. I gather, they think, they can pay for it. Alright. But let there be justice for life in flesh and blood "under the sun, moon and stars," sings Jimmy Cliff. We know flesh and blood will not inherit the kingdom, but while we're in it the spirit of the living God anoints us with means to an abundant life. The Healer said I came that you might have life, constantly aware of inequities in the world between those who had the means to healing and those who lined hallways having no means, asking for cure, crying out with their eyes lifted up, some on their knees, others standing, few walking, so many, so many slain in the spirit. Everyday Mama in the throes of the spirit, wailed: thy will be done on Earth as it is in Heaven. On Earth! Justice is done in Heaven. What prevents, or has prevented justice from being done on Earth?

More than thirty years ago, in the heated 1970s, Reggae singer Jimmy Cliff arduously desired his peace not through the eye of a protestant ethic but under the Sun Moon and Stars -- within visible, tangible reality evident in his Creator's faith and works! Thing is too, even those who claim to stand for justice sometimes do not hear its cry, nor can they identify with the spot from which it springs. Silence. Justice, my old man said; that great war of justice will be fought between rich and poor, between North and south and there will be blood!

CHAPTER 31

Bingo!

Once parents deposited these precious troves, these edifying codes of wisdom in their children's thinking. While their meanings were not immediately Unraveled, as the child grew the code was gradually broken. Significance of the sayings found reference in the child's world. So much of the counsel was basic, authenticating the brilliance of these people. The war of justice will be between rich and poor, North and South, he said. He is not here to see its unraveling, but by God, from his village in this globe, he was right on. He was, and in many ways still is, my philosophy teacher. My Mother rooted me. This is not to say that philosophy is not grounded deep -- we applied it, and I believe that mama was, toward the application side of the philosophy continuum with special attention given to everyday existence, feeding, clothing, shelter, education, sense of belonging. Our Mother made sure that everyone had clothing for occasions, walked without dragging our feet carried our bodies upright. Dignity. It is left to the children to stretch out everyday learned simplicities. Every occasion carries an attitude. Don't be sloppy in your gait. You might have taken it for granted and it seems a great leap but the spinal cord connects brain. Their sayings and requirements contain seeds of victory and survival, traces of sound financial discipline, healthy living anecdotes, management of time and physical energy resources. We have to return to basics. Take the simplicity route, I hear my Father say, his genetics cool. Culture I. Culture your body -- a great sentient, responsive teacher prepared for you. Strengthen what you have now. Strengthen what remains.

Recollection of childhood life-culture takes us playfully, to and beyond the threshold of our liberation search. We recorded events voices faces experiences largely unaware of the process. Deposits made into our accounts are bursting into sizeable amounts, nutritive narratives. Those seeds have been dead for too long buried too deep from those who sought the substance of our dreams. Mama would say this is the season, this is the time. Our parents knew how to protect us. Our West Indian forefathers and foremothers were no simpletons balancing struggle over time. We might not have noticed it, but there is always a place for us, in us to be revealed only to us to be broken by our hand. Think of it. Much to the surprise of those who thought us poor after their linear measure, we eat and drank and slept and danced and played and ran and ran for miles and miles in open air pure clean unadulterated unpolluted, drank unbottled spring water. We did not have the quality highways bridges and cars skymimickers and sprawling shopping zones. At Christmas time every home was rich.

Collectively we constitute a sort of mythological movement living each day as if it were the last, yet not knowing the significance of last and first in this unfolding panorama that is life. In the midst of our joy there was disease and death though the latter was highly infrequent. A death stunned community. Grandparents died but seldom did the young. Death by vehicular accident was rare because there were fewer vehicles. A fight seldom led to killing. An illness in adults encountered a tough defense system. Children did not have television to pattern their responses on. Freddie carrying a gun was known in community. Knives were used as working instruments. We knew that those who died would not return. We saw crying relatives go back to life dressing in black, in subdued colors of mourning for weeks even months. Even our hurting, in spite of its psychological cuts bore sense of wonder.

Sadness tugs gently. Its light presence reminds me of Life's abundant gift of emotions, so ripe in Mothers. Mothers understood disappearances, wearing mourning with humility. Mothers have had to come to terms with departures for millennia; have had to let go off their babies by way of nature's rhythms. Those new-borns left their bodies. They leave their eco-protection as soon as nature has structured their breathing apparatus to readiness. Many children would go on to live with their parents into adulthood, and it is true that West Indian/ Caribbean Mothers are known to express reluctance over letting their children go. Yet many do not like being inconveniences to their children and extended family in old age. I heard of a great meditation teacher who was diagnosed in his elder years as having cancer. An entire movement was moved by news of his condition. On his advice the best oncologist and other persons in the field were brought in. The diagnosis was the same. The teacher stood within himself and asked that he be given water. He had water for the next 32 days and died peacefully. He did not want to be an inconvenience. When this story was told to me by Dominican meditation teacher Anthony Toulon, I realized that in some circumstances a person can culture dying -- brave ones choose a route to the same common end. Those, like our meditation teacher, who go deliberately quietly leaving behind a record of their slow passage can tell us about the many mansions entered into along the way to healing. I ask gently, would death be the only medium to this house or would its doors be open to the living righteous? Long night's reasoning, I suggest. Those who die peacefully may well have cultured breath's motions rising, falling like tides, leaving for us all traces of transcendental beauty, physiological and anatomical potential. Silence. And what of those who do not die quietly who in depression take their lives? We call it untimely unfortunate and ask why didn't she find someone to talk with. It might have been her time, sadly, if not mysteriously unfolded by her own hands. There is that moment no existing knowledge predicts, describes, captures, or holds minor traces of. Not even those who culture dying know its arrival. It is a private meeting. It is frightening to me to write this. I do not even know the course of my own life. I cannot know the path my death will take. But I am acquainted now with a silent place that knows humanity the way we do not know ourselves. In the language of the entertainer it is out of this world. There are those, in the restlessness of imminent death, those having that opportunity, who take prayer to the point where they are prayed until the unknown second arrives. Is this innocence, or possession by a force showing the way, cutting off community and loved-ones? The homo sapien is indeed a unique mammal: it cultures dying. If it has the intelligence to end this stage in flesh and blood then it is inherent in flesh and blood to begin life. If the human has the capacity to begin the process of ending life, then it has the capacity to advance life indeed to draw principles of rebirth into life, knowing its wellbeing and longevity discourse path. Significant to note this: the Meditation Teacher left a remarkable record of his gradual transformation until that gentler moment inscribed in his heart, known only to the universe, to his Creator.

Is the human being a mere vessel in whom all that is deposited all that is known has its time, season and fructifying purpose? So indeed he knew my name before I was conceived is genuine. What was that name and was it the one given to me by my Father, agreed upon by my Mother? How could a Caribbean child primarily of African descent have carried a name composed of Jewish Portuguese and British, while there is a name-sound that he was known by? Listen. Would be interesting to know and hear what Jesus' name was in Hindi. You ask why select Christ Jesus? So many Latin American males carry the name Jesus. It even sounds attractively powerful in Spanish. If the Je was pronounced in the style of French, that too would have a quality of majesty. I've often thought that the sus following Je misses only an I to make it je suis, I am, in French. But then I have to separate je and suis. In English, the name is soft, you see. But I gather it depends on whether it is being said by an American evangelist or an Episcopalian.

I know pastors who close their eyes when saying that name, others who tremble. Truly, I find myself interested in this person. How could a man have calmed seas rose the dead make the blind see change water into wine healed a woman with an issue of blood caused a fig tree to die stuck back a man's ear when it was cut off prophesied so clearly stages of this world, died, said he would rise from the dead, did, had the lion's courage to say that we live with him wherever he is, wherever he left his body and blood. Heia, he said he left the Holy Spirit as a deposit. A deposit? In lieu of what? A larger amount? amazing! Just when we thought it was over, he said he would come again. Bingo! Is there not something amazing about this? Aren't the living creatures of Revelation more awesome than Satan? Can you imagine a battle in Hell, vibration pouring out from the throne of the Most High and the chant, the chant is ceaseless and hypnotic silence. My God, the silent gaze lifting hell's flight armory like tea-cups is piercing and terrible. Then those four creatures with eyes all over lift their twenty-four wings to cast out the enemy. Silence!

CHAPTER 32

Love of a Knowing Being

I have arrived at a terribly awesome place. I am overwhelmed by power of reverent fear. I must conclude that where I am is where I'm supposed to be. Whatever my circumstances I give thanks. I am a vessel.

The door-bell rings. I open to our daughter. She calls her Mother regarding afternoon arrangements, proceeds to the kitchen and begins to warm some food. She asks whether I would like something to eat. Not only did I feel emptied. It was customary for her to offer or ask.

The fork is lifted unusually heavily to my mouth. I feel like I am about to drink medicine I don't like but is good for my healing. Nothing is wrong with the food or the kind gesture of a Daughter to her Father. The heeling flows from inside but all that is in me does not drink.

Flood my mind and heart and will, God of my salvation. Her offering has stimulated my whole. The flood may not be tasty to the mouth but it is good for the stomach. Bitterness will give way to spring water the quality gushing out of a Dominican rock body. The hand lifting the fork is not mine. The colorful presentation dislodged tiny chips of chemical rock beyond one single sense. I am thankful. The delight is slow in its own time touching, soothing its chosen meridians. I am helpless on this mode of transportation -- its route I barely know its twists and bends are surprises. Its highways are for miles as if along a path of millions of neurons and alleys of intestinal easiness. Yes. My organs are covered in the mess of sin. Pour out your spirit. Anoint. Cross the frontiers of the iniquity of my youth. Cause me to care the gifts you gave to me. Let me see beauty and truth in my children purity in their Mothers eyes. Let go doubt. Let go anxiety. Free me from the things I think I know. Expand my steel will in the Fire of your Love. Communication? Go to your closet. Remove the anger that strikes your heart to dying. Roll out the lies you've been told, your strata of hatreds, your geology of beliefs. Learn the power in waiting and gifts in prayer intangibles moving to action, to your will over distance, over time having no geographic nor topographic preferences. Walk yourself with confidence: you will not stumble. Take receive from the knowing being inside. Yes Mama.

CHAPTER 33

On Returning from Dominica's Capital

Two days after our Mother was buried, rain fell on the land. I was in Dominica's capital Roseau. The night was a deep dark and wonderful silence over one of the world's most salubrious island environments. Stillness was alive though most would have been in by one in the morning. From Carla's house on the hill at Goodwill, I could hear Roseau River talking, running to pass beneath two bridges then, as it made its deposits in its sea account. The Roseau river was not as strong as it used to be thirty years ago when I was a young boy at the Dominica Grammar School. Deforestation had deprived it of its myriad churns.

Rain kept the dogs quiet. It's not the kind of rain you find in the morning's wet. It's the kind you hear on the roof that reaches a threshold in sound to craftily fade into dawn. Watching it fall alone left me longing. By daybreak Saturday the market-place hummed with voices color and aroma of earth-drawn food. To the north of the market's colorful fresh-food display, ran the Roseau River West to the Caribbean Sea blue to silver in morning's sunlight. Hundreds buy and sell in this place where class disappears. Basille peppermint rosemary parsley jellynuts watermelons carrots, green yellow red white purple flowers, breadfruits breadnuts dasheen were in abundance though much less than what it used to be ten years ago. Still at the peak of mourning I walked the market's circumference to feel its Dominican originality and simplicity, inhale the aroma of its cinnamon and bayleaf, buy its arrowroot and farines. As light stretched elegantly into the Roseau Valley, I caught an early ride up north to Portsmouth traveling along the cool coast of stratified rocks cacti and shrubs hardy vegetation, wrought in Caribbean Sea blast blisteringly in August when remains of each passing storm lingered, when heat starred in the drama of midday sun. I thought of thousands living in villages close to the sea, how their community spirit almost always made me believe that they would be safe by the sheer forces of bonding. They were generally settled at the western foot of the most mountainous island in the Eastern Caribbean. The Changing world environment posed such a threat to these coastal communities populating islands states, I thought. Up north we went by way of Salisbury, Coulibistrie, Colihaut, Bioche, Dublanc, Ti-Bay -- for those who like British and French sounding remains in names. We descended Espanol, headed up the gradient and, wow! These mountains to the North and East rose magnificently above the green spread as we approached Ross University School of Medicine. What a refreshing site. When we entered Glanvillia, the Caribbean Sea to the West seemed like it needed a bridge into the distance where the Sun would finally descend.

Portsmouth just under thirty miles from the capital was soaked and washed by the northern moving rainfall. The soil was logged, the Air clean. A few days before we had put away a body. I'm back to the general space, its emotions, its weeping. As I approached my sister's house, the reality of absence hit me. Her breath is in the Air around us. This spirit this wind this pneuma is in our domain. She might have figured in the rain silver like her hair, only that I didn't see she herself smiling from behind beads of sunlit water.

Most times we see what we want to see. This strength of perception has not been explored sufficiently for use in a positive way though the gurus have told us when you see it on water as you think it, it becomes reality. There is spirit in whatever is sustainable.

Who will never leave me is the presence of the person I expect to meet in that room each time I enter. I gather our conversations were meaningful, poignant enough to have me weeping. I could not help not believing how the seeds of a spectral continuity were being sown. The power in her simplicity astounded me. Still, it is her honest truth dipping into her self drawing out the closest she could come to what she felt and envisioned that captivates in my present tense. Truly, my lover was gone. This one of all the others baffles me. As soon as I was fit to run she set me free. She needed to know that I could take care of myself. She didn't possess me though if anyone had to she would be the most rightful. I came out of her. I took shape in her even as she chanted. The body that aged by way of its stubbornness its silences, its pleasantness was once my house my source my resting place my oasis my spring water my restoration. Breath hovered over its waters still unbroken by the light, to be broken soon in original light. Wow. That flesh would have decomposed a bit, yielded to bacteria leaving a world of form as we know it. The heart that suffered hurt would have been picked at, its passion and desire for life ended in the flesh. All its doubts terrors uncertainties and troubles would have commenced releasing their physical character to the Earth and Air in these times of unmatched attractions unyoked liaisons.

I feel the emptying an unfurling of a new standard and it is not as sorrow. It is respect for each second, for more minute time distribution segments, as breath finds its arteries. I hear clamor and rush -- the world's most perceptive talking about a brink. I hear no irregular heartbeats should be troubling. I hear do not be unduly saddened over a departed soul and the course of its journey. Tears are not forever. In fact, the Canadian singers remind us that tears will never be enough. When you face it, active memory cleanses consciousness. Cry if you have to remember if you have to. Those are places you pass and they will leave seeds on your clothing sand in your shoes laughter's divine energy in your head. Be patient with yourself, counsels the desiderata. The wild calls to the wild. An explicit deliverance is being consummated.

Hey, a sacrifice of joy acquires shape in water and Fire. Life flows on to life. Life would stop in motion to cuddle banks, tease soaked leaves from their selfless rest, shift pebbles slide and roll stones. Move on. Moon's light would have fallen pellucidly on Water and the Sun warm its banks and vegetation. The Siffleur Montagne whistles its random melody its sweet similarity to life's ups and downs and the futility of death's struggle. Yet randomness is only one of its styles. There is silence wherein there is no measure of Love's symphony. Leaves pores climax. Dew comes. A branch may burst from its stem and echo along the surface of a surrounding Fresh Water Lake. From a window lovers kiss, remains of sunlight's ecstasy brown on their dopamine-laden faces. What pleasure. Move on.

Older women met in the town who could be my Mother are telling me to take care of myself. Though I appreciated their sympathies, I began to get that unsettling feeling that there were others who did not really care and still others who think us vulnerable now that the Mother-figure is gone. Truly, she symbolizes protector. This is the case in every known culture. One friend told me in Caribbean culture too there are families who reveal their true colors after parents are dead. All along we didn't like you but Mama was around. What could Mama do. Mama's prayer works. Like the other women she made it to the church and lit her candle. She could, like every other woman chant the Hail Mary and knew declarative power in the Novenas. She could request a service for her children take them to the priest. Some Mothers dared to meet the obeahman on behalf of their children. Mama never did. Rome sometimes had to give way to Africa or blend with it! Yes, Mother knew the secret herb plant and flower seasons and tides to apply to her children's life. She had kept the secrets of healing passed on by her Mother and Grandmother, yet glaucoma could not be caught. Grandmother used to tell me, one drop of iodine in milk clears the lungs. Ooops, they concocted. Even while Mother could not trap glaucoma in its early and late stages, whenever Mama said don't worry, it always seemed like the matter was closed from here. With a few words she could drive troubles away. What a psychologist. Mothers had to be psychologist, physiologist, clinical hypnotherapist, healer, nurse, economist, nutritionist, disciplinarian, comforter, and most times, she just had to be there. Mama had to be a resting place a defense in our time of childhood mythology, superstition and economic change. When a child was born all holes in the wooden house were blocked to keep out spirits or drafts, some say. Observe the synonymity in wind draft spirit. None is visible. They buried the navel-string under a tree believing that as the tree grew the child would also. I guess the cord feeds -- the root, receives water and warmth all year round. It breathes too. Indeed the child grows in the spirit of the plant. Any parent who chose to bury a navel-string under a banana tree in the days when banana was king made, it seems, a wise economic decision. It made short-term sense. Each fortnight there was a return on sales and bananas threw out fruit within six months anyway. In a London office men and women gathered to determine their buying price, their tentacles extending into Jamaica St. Lucia St. Vincent Grenada and Dominica. National media controlled by governments in these territories would announce that bananas were being received this week and the amount being paid per pound. While a pound of sugar would sell for fifty cents, a pound of bananas -- laden with calcium, iron, magnesium, phosphorous, potassium and a load of vitamins -- was being bought for ten cents, thirteen cents and so on. I used to think they were selling for us. Those horticulturists in England were masters at extracting value, greater still at justifying it numerically. The trade nevertheless fed thousands of households mostly those of single Mothers.

Hundreds and hundreds of women in those islands ran on peers carrying that "green gold" on their heads to lighters to be towed by tugs to that white ship. Their names were indicative of a shipping lexicon. They were Geest Bay, Geest Land, Geest Haven, Geest Star and Geest Port. There might have been a Geest Crest. I knew them well anchored in the natural harbor so close to shore so deep too deep, too calm to be disturbed, transformed. The women carried pouches tied to their waists in which they deposited the copper-colored ticket, one to each banana carried. They ran with some splendid bunches strong black women young and old fit and lean. In those days there was no news of high blood pressure. Miscarriages were rare unless a woman of bourgeois orientation decided to abort to protect her image. Community was never to know her as a fornicator nor recall that she carried a bastard. Those who carried bananas did not hide. They gave birth. They had sex. Two decades later those who carried would be proud and those who aborted lived and died lonely lives in big houses with no one to care for, no child to feed, so much food to throw. Choice can sometimes lead to oblivion.

CHAPTER 34

Mama's Capital Base

From the dawn of the 60s to the late 80s banana was lucrative business. However, by the mid-80s, those women on jetties began disappearing. Conveyor belts were on the run. Mental arithmetic was already replaced by adding machines and large-faced calculators. Ships with those huge white bellies were leaving, their crew waving goodbyes, but we did not notice. I pray she did not bury my placenta under a banana tree! From its nutrients in root and shoot to stem branches and fruit the bunch is cut. She anticipated its loading. She will never know how or where they are offloaded sold or converted. She will never know the real profits extracted from an acclaimed fair trade, neither will she see them on display in supermarkets by hands that did not plant them. If only hands retrieving those nutritive candy-blessed hands from refrigerated shelves recognized those who took it off the tree loaded it and ran with it with hands on either side or, just one holding it secure over time, time and a half, double time. If only they knew how much these women carriers diligently handled the bunch, how each farmer cuddles each green hand!

They dressed to receive their pay, those women carriers. Yes, pay day was the big day. I think Mama knew how much each woman received having prepared each woman's pay packet. She could safely assess the quality of life of the average household in the town of Portsmouth and its adjoining communities. Thirty, forty and sixty dollars was a bit of money then and the pay packets were received with pride. The women were called by name. One friend intimated, reminded me that usually the pay packet was already gone by the time they received it: credit. It was alright. There was extended family support. Truth is, so many women came back each fortnight to make just enough to cover expenses in the fashion of confident faith actors. In time they would learn to push their bodies passed its pain into rhythmic joy of collective carrying action, to earn that extra over and beyond expenses. They inherited the culture of servicing a sub, thereby pooling and equally distributing financial resources over set time-frames. Mothers subs saved many lives. Even in the world's largest financial centers, Caribbean women still practice subbing.

After years of concealed profits the British horticulturists left those natives in abeyance; any effort by them to be innovative in marketing, partially dysfunctional. They should not find out that side -- if only they had done marketing for themselves. Nature screamed relief. Humans screamed crisis.

CHAPTER 35

Beyond Capital

I return now to that world underlying modes of production equity and balanced distribution of forces. I return to that reciprocity and unspoken regard for the other. I return to a life greater than this sojourn on a ship more majestic. You mourn my passing but soon you will dance. You weep now, your stomach throwing up waves of wails that salt your eyes with reddening rings. you will surely laugh. When a deep depression holds your thoughts in ice, you will find the warmth of your soul anointing. You'll be led away from recollections of failure and doubt. When you see the generation after you walking in innocence and justice, you will whisper a prayer in hope that your nightmare will become their enriched sociology, your darkened clothes their rainbow, your fasted flesh their quickening. Your primitive heart will know the seasons and times, rise and fall of tides and depth secrets in darkness will be revealed to you. You have a well-equipped institution lit inside your heart, just beyond your usual smiling reach, your pleasantries. You shall know its kindled flame and respect its anchored dwelling place. Sow patience and you will reap infinite patience. Give when you see the need and rejoice in the gifts in your hands knowing they too are outstretched.

What about blood. Is this dried up conjointly? Or does it live in remaining rivers in all forms of living things. What you embrace today you may refrain from embracing tomorrow. Every living thing has its purpose. Let this be. There is a time when a child does not want to be held, does not need to be held but allowed to run and be guided by its own internal wonder-map. There are times when that child needs to be held and caressed. It was in the hand that his bones were nourished, his and her nerve tissue soothed. It was in the tender stroking of the forehead and tapping massages to the spine. It was in the compassionate closeness with which Mother carried us against her body. It was hushed finger across the lips, warm breasts giving rest, nutrition play bytes and sleeping space. Some people are better seen and known from a distance.

It will not be sufficient to present a chronology of events while the spirit of the text harks to another time, another place a greener landscape another state. No individual thing is permanent except in a collective zone yet, we concede each time place landscape and state has its symmetry and bounce its waterfalls and plotted highways its religion and creed.

This house has no clear shape no walls now. Here no one defends no one offends. This house protects yet has no roofing. My God. I am at the well. I am tired. Need a hand. One is stretched out to me. There are lots and lots of children here. Many know me and sing my name in a welcoming chant. One thing I always desired of the Lord was to dwell in his house all the days of my Life to behold his beauty get to know the wonders of his temple. Through faith I had glimpses of it on Earth and now I have the perfect view. Once I was blind and now I see. Let the children come to me, Christ Jesus said. They are heavenly, the free-flowing in thought and play. They are the pure in heart, the undefiled, those who do not judge. She was received. Yes, Could I say that Zicack's Earth community of saints prayed for her to be received? Could I safely say that libations directed ancestral spirits to her and together they resorted to banks beside still waters? What beautiful presumptuousness. A glimpse of what we lived through, helps in understanding our Mothers faith at work.

CHAPTER 36

Thrills in Our Childhood

For the 50s generation the 60s represented an age of innocence and innovation.

We had musicians boxers cricketers singers actors netballers footballers strong carnival revelers fantastic costume designers. We were not just design-savvy. Today it would've been a multi-billion dollar business. There was craft an style intricate patterns and color explosions. The SensÉ/Sensay is today still indigenous to Dominica's carnival. Costumes were constructed using cloth crepe tin rubber bottle-covers satin card sisal plastic rope. There were those who came out with horns and others with big-heads -- oversized designed heads, terrifying children. Animation did not hit big-screens yet. It was being manufactured in yards and brought to streets in marches in rows and columns on an island discovered better by the knowledgeable.

Ten members of a satin-dressed carnival group would appear from the distant hill in diverse colors in a meandering formation. It was fantasy under sunlight! It is a fantasy that requires documentation of its own. There was no formal culture or entertainment industry and such talent, such beauty was relegated to ranks of bad boys and girls. The latter was the chantrelle, the woman who produced a serious mas. See clearly how times have changed, or metamorphosized. Today, costumes of those bad Dominican boys and girls are in demand from carnival lovers all over the world -- at each major festival on the island of Dominica, whether Carnival or Independence celebrations. This realization took almost forty years and that too is too long. It is something that invites our consideration. Those designers, those revelers were not perceived as constituting actors in a lucrative industry; when the season was over, we had to wait another year for another glamourous appearance. But let us not forget, they pleased us and brought us joy.

Too many of those young and old men who worked Carnival drums in 1965 -- among them, those born in the early 1940s -- passed away in the 90s without a drum on their coffins, goat-skin wrapping their waists. Amazing. Thousands reveled in their rhythms. They made the death announcements, not the headlines. We need a list of drummers today, and when anyone of them dies, whether old or young, we must, from the highest social and political level celebrate their passing with a number of drums equal to their age. But, I gather this soul-filled idea does not build a bridge. As for musicians, this requires its own lyrics stretched out on separate rivers, between pillars of Fire. Musicians intercept, interrupt injustices. There is so much to tell others about us.

During my years in Canada one student asked whether where I came from people really lived in trees. In 1979, economics Nobel Laureate St. Lucian, Sir Arthur Lewis, reminded the world that the Caribbean had and has a high standard of living. My friend would not have known that since she conceded living in trees was how they were taught to perceive us or for that matter the only visual representation they had of us in so-called poor countries. Unlike us, they had lice maybe even more. They suffered through all the poxes mumps and epidemics of the time. It was only in the 90s that the cumulative lifestyle diseases, the environment disaster phenomenon began to pinch us frequently. We did not rush to deposit our elders in hospices in a frantic bid to accelerate their death, inherit their property. We never had to put them out in the cold or dark because there was not enough to feed the children; on Sundays they were assured of visits by the extended clan.

Thinking in the yesterday space is an act of friendliness among thoughts and their energies. I just remembered that in the 1960s, the government of Dominica contracted my Mother as a census worker. Usually, she'd take me with her. We walked through Dominica's northern communities of Cottage and Gillette, along hillsides down valleys into quaint yet neatly kept yards and houses. The word landscaping was called weeding then. Tell you, in communities we visited, those scape-artists used a cutlass to shape spaces overlooking the sea and breast of mini-mountains. My Mother was forever teaching me by word or deed. It was either observation of her soft-spoken nature, in drawing out information from respondents or just the ease with which she got along with village, agriculture people working as an official. Didn't know it, but Mother's census-taking days marked my introduction to the long interview as method in social sciences -- the germinative days of my field-work. Living in trees? This same woman who interacted with fishing and farming communities, kept a small garden, but never really liked agriculture, though throughout my years as a boy we kept cattle, fowls, sheep. People of my childhood days cultured cattle mules goats rabbits pigeons pigs sheep and fowls. We did not refer to fowls as birds. In fact it was common for each household to keep fowls. We knew the egg had come when the cackling began. In addition to food supplies drawn from our small garden supplemented by gifts and purchases from the extended family, Mama believed that fowls, pigs, cows, goats and sheep held value. They had to be cared. Animals are such great friends, though I only knew this in part then.

Undoubtedly, our early childhood practices allow us today, a quality of sophistication that has only just begun its millennium oeuvre among island musicians, painters, dancers, actors, athletes, healers, scientists, teachers, mathematicians, physicists, physicians, therapists, florists, herbalists, architects, environmentalists, geologists, lawyers, bankers, leaders, community police officers, farmers, fishers, culinary experts, manufacturers, entrepreneurs, midwives, nurses. Yes, we the emergent, the surfacers, lived in a loaded environment, protected, guided by our Mothers.

CHAPTER 37

Figures in Our World and Underworld

In addition to everyday economic activity, the 50s and 60s in our island community were days of superstition and fragments of wisdom. In the yard of every soucouyant or those whom we cared to call witch, grew a diversity of plants, fruits and herbs. While they were not the only ones who grew herbs and medicinal plants they were more likely to keep what others did not have. They were the mystic women about whom numerous stories were told. They were believed to fly, some as far as over the "channel" between Dominica and its northern neighbor of Guadeloupe. It was said that they decorated and mounted broomsticks and flew. Hail! Some were reported to change their skins or change from human being to birds and other animals. They wore dark clothing attended church religiously and yet had few friends. The inner sections of their houses were dark since windows were kept permanently shut.

Too many children were frightened by soucouyants who extended a strong cultural politics over a young small-town population. But to be honest, there was something about those alleged soucouyants that

I liked even as a boy. Maybe it was the mystery which surrounded their lives, their aloneness, their silence some of them. I remember trying talking with one who looked at me with such sternness, that I never tried again. Were they really evil? What was it that they did, that most women did not dare to do? Why did they grow so many plants and herbs around their houses? Why were their eyes so bright, flashing to the slightest sound? Tell you, Mama in her living days had lots to interpret. When she did successfully, all fears dissipated.

Quite apart from having to provide for her children, quite apart from her struggles with early shadowy challenges of glaucoma, she had a cantankerous neighbor known as a soucouyant. The call to love your neighbor as yourself was critically real. I saw the acclaimed soucouyant unfold. I remember she was the odd unfriendly kind. She would begin mumbling to herself if water was thrown from our kitchen into our yard. A visitor to our house drew her attention. She would peep from the spaces in the boards forming her outside kitchen. I gather we were under constant surveillance. This was my Mother's neighbor visible at daybreak before she left for work and audible at dusk.

The trouble as I understood it then was over two feet of land running less than fifty yards between our houses. Land disputes are terribly long and most times futile. She died before my Mother leaving the two feet between us and all the fertile ground on which her house once stood.

What comes to mind most readily is my Mother's overcoming. Each day she had to rise over above a quarrelsome storm. Our Mother would say, "the Earth is the Lord's and the fullness thereof." Still, I believe our neighbor might have been a good person who became an antagonist as she grew older. The soucouyants were so far from the norm of caring. They simply could not change their skin into kindness and labels increased.

As children we learnt the immense trouble that land disputes brought and the futility of the battles. We also learnt that quarrels consume energy. Too much productive energy was spent aligning with mischief. There are wicked people: those who admit unfriendliness, those who started off in search of something and lost their way. Human history is replete with lost and found stories. Only Berger et al could have realized fertility in a homeless mind. In spiritual circles one could say I was lost and now I'm found. There was the sheep that went astray, the one from the one hundred. The shepherd went in search of it and brought it home. Yes mama. Sometimes one has to get lost to be found. Sometimes too, Papa humored seriously, the only way to get out of trouble is to go into more trouble. Putting all things aside, as Mama used to say, there is a virtue called forgiveness. When the dust is settled on both sites and sides of the wall the emotional strain, the loss over struggles for land is tremendous. Hate seems to shoot almost genetically giving the impression that such is the nature of the entire human condition. Boyhood innocence living in me is distraught by this sting of advanced differences plaguing the human race. But I guess by dint of a rhythmic cadence I am called to remember the good, light side issuing simultaneously. I choose. I put all things aside. I present presence and find joy in communicating now in spite of all that might have transpired before this here.

I recall another old woman. The old woman who kept herbs and plants in her yard for application to the sick was revered and called Dada. She was the busy mystic woman who could not simply stand in the shadows of the temple, neither could any yard be so territorialized that she would not enter at will at any time. Dadas cured everything from colds to fevers to strains which we called bless. Dada cured these strains right down to children who behaved as if possessed by a jombi. Those were the children who stole compulsively or got into fights frequently. Then there were those who needed 'bush tea', those who had an ailment that never went away, you know, a permanent flu, running nose, cough, whizzing. Every Caribbean yard had a Dada. Children were sometimes referred to her because they just drifted aimlessly as if compelled by an unexercised force. They were described as having dwiv, denoting a drift -- being constantly transported into trouble involuntarily. Children who walked and walked and seldom were at their home -- a sort of wanderer -- were called dwivayèz. Thing is, if as a boy, you didn't do some dwivÉing, you'd really not know too much of the environment, its play and river-spots, its river basèns, its fresh crop of mangoes, soursop or papaya. I believe, that those compulsive dwivayez or drifters, knew what they were doing. There was the odd aimless, but most were simply hanging out. Home was in many cases a small place anyway, entered when it was time to sleep. Eating was done in the yard or outside kitchen.

Dadas spotted the sick, the jombi-possessed and perceived wanderer, from a distance. Not only could they massage. They would draw down swellings and extricate whizzing. Their fingers carried codes of a healing energy tradition that can only be traced to Africa. Through their acts of healing Dadas praise God for good fruits of knowledge extending from generation to generation of those who love and obey those commandments passed on by Moses and later summarized by Christ Jesus. Love. Dadas did not only love their neighbors. They were responsible for the well-being of their offspring. No one told them that was their lot: they took it upon themselves as if chosen to do just that. They were responding to an inner dynamic, an inherent cultural tendency. The gift in their hands was evident in most Mothers of the time though not as pronounced. Yes, the women of my childhood kept secrets of healing but the range of infections were few. Children were taken to hospital only in extreme cases of injury, pain and unease. Our Mothers were occupied with other working matters and over time, relinquished that knowledge as mainstream medicine dug in. That burst of healing insight would emerge only in times of emergency, on special occasions. Moreover, after a while children themselves began to know what to take for the flu or fever. It took the Mother to know however that the soursop (graviola guanabana) leaf when drawn contributed to a child's perfect rest. God grant Mothers insight knowledge in this epoch of nightmares and insomnia!

I believe doctors found good talking with these alternative women and paradoxically the doctors might have been the only ones willing or able to have a free conversation with both Dadas and soucouyants. Lawyers and priests made soucouyants uncomfortable. As for children, they stayed away from the perceived evil. A few rebel boys and girls were brave enough to call them soucouyant to their face and the one who felt accused or guilty would curse usually in KwÉyòl, one of Dominica's languages -- the only language that could deliver real gut meaning. It is today still the language of the Dominican seer and obeahman. The latter beats his Tarot pack and delivers his hermeneutics in KwÉyòl!

The 1960s were therefore bizarre, yet wonderful times for the innocent. We danced as much as we went in early. This was not because Mama required that we get in the house before six though this was evident to us. Stories abounded about men with one leg who stood at road corners with a carpenter's rule in hand. Horses galloped through streets after midnight. We were not to be found outside after midnight, but arrival of darkness meant the presence of frightening forces, half humans, even those who transformed themselves into animals. If anything, I would have thought after the third hour to be more frightening but after twelve was good enough to scare any child. Street lights were five hundred yards apart. Darkness was thick. Shadows of a banana tree rocking in the Wind could create images of human effigies, half-human figures, sometimes with or without heads, with or without arms, no eyes, just swaying in the wind, in motion, yet not in motion like a banana tree under cloud and moonlight shifting.

There was the jombi. The jombi was not a soucouyant whom we saw -- having shape and form. While I referred to the jombi as a ghost, my friend Philbert Aaron told me the jombi was a spirit. Holy Ghost and Holy Spirit are interchangeable though different from the ghost of a jombi. The jombi could have possessed someone. A person could carry a jombi on them. In this case it required what we call and exorcism. It read as an evil spirit. Jombis were invisible. In fact a colonial absentee owner could be seen as a jombi and a nation which did not know itself could be in the grips of a jombi. Dr. Philbert Aaron a Dominican from the community of Lagoon, in the town of Portsmouth is likely to advance this metaphor into the regions of national identity and the spirit of belonging to a particular nation-state, class, color creed. The issue of spirit has been contained in capitalism to mean energy, vision. Just imagine, Dr. Aaron, a discourse on the jombi of capitalism! The implications for education policy and leadership are crucial!

What could have been a positive interpretation of a mythology became an evil thus a fear and a rejection that now struggles to accept an ecology of forest trees market notions of possession and passion. What might have been a Holy Spirit what we sang about and were told to look forward to had an apparent opposite which in our language was negative. It was used as an instrument of fear. I suggest that it was drawn out of our own beliefs and truly, might have been introduced as a guardian angel or friend to children of an African tradition, albeit twisted in the vice of a dominant religion. What still amazes me is that the men -- the dyab, diable, devil -- those partial forms at the four corner-road were most times described by locals as white, though images in pictures in nearly all houses where they existed showed a devil as black and a white angel throwing him into hell-fire. An ideological battle must have developed using images in the Catholic Church: consistently they represented Christ, the Apostles and Saints as white. In another religious movement, Not only was the devil black; he carried a tail indicating an incomplete human or animal and always, always with Fire in his eyes. Remember hell! Hell was a place of Fire. Years later, when I became a man, my Mother told me that this was not the modern image, face. Satan she said was a handsome, sweet-smiling man with all his teeth! Deception.

The diabless, the female devil was described as a seductive-looking woman. A man would be driving in his car late at night, only to find a woman along the way asking for a ride. Being male, he saw an opportunity, never questioning what such a beautiful woman "doing" on the road at this time all alone. He stopped for her. Along the way, while seated in his vehicle, one of her legs begins to be transformed. By the time she got out, he observes fearfully that she had the leg of a hoofed creature and that of a woman. Mi vitesse! All along she kept smiling smoothly. Little information was known regarding the diablesse's power, though her mystery charm was renown.

The soucouyant lived in community, while the jombi, dyab/diable and diablesse resided in the under-world. In spite of this hierarchy, we knew those accused. They lived over and above our religious simplicity having retained a knowledge that most of our parents no longer recognized. We the boys and girls, knew those in community rumored to have relations with the world of the hidden; we said they were dealing.

Mr. Andrew, Mister dealing. This could mean that he wore a big ring of Solomon or David. Ironic, isn't it? These were wise men, who when presented to us by those who taught religion, did not mystify, had no dark struggles, engaged no evil spirits. Pleasures of innocence, I imagine. The dealer could disappear, turn into a dog. It was always a dog, man's best animal friend. When the dealer rode he used a horse, usually and intriguingly, a white one. Those girls and boys -- dramatic story-tellers -- threw in dragging chains for terror's sake. Horse and rider were met at the corner of a road, standing still. It was again, always at the corner of the road, what the older folk called the four-road. Indecision. doubt. In this square, or rectangle was a force, a hidden force that a few men in villages and small towns learned to harness. These practitioners existed. They would not be subject to church doctrine or subtle fear strategies. Books on mysticism were ubiquitous as a sort of affront to established religious thought. The intensity of the tug-of-war between orthodoxy and indigenous religious ideologies, rose and fell as economy and values changed. As power shifted so did influence find new force, authorities new clients and willing subjects. Many were willing simply to make a living. There were those however, who dared to challenge dogma and the oversimplified body and blood hell-fire sin and punishment.

Despite the statues and their pale cold passion fire, the home-spun stories presented no color concept of God Christ or the Saints. Prayer was to God through Christ Jesus. God rode the wind over Iowa as much as over Haiti. It did not matter whether God was referred to as he. All prayer was made through Jesus Christ. He was the King of the Jews and though we children had never seen a modern Jew it did not matter. We were taught that Jesus lived in our hearts. This place of eternal rest, this one who we were asked to cast our burdens on who now lives in Heaven lives in our hearts. This Christ, this Spirit living in my heart is dangerously wonderful. The man who gave John the Revelation lives in my heart. The Word made Flesh lives in my heart. The Word that was with God in the beginning lives in my heart. Heavy for a child! Is it not? He was and is leader in God's government in the departments of health economics politics Defense Human and community development communications and planning. Heavier still.

Let's not leave out Justice! He went to culture a place. We were taught that he lives in Heaven. Heaven is in our hearts. The Kingdom of Heaven is within you. What wonder when we were told too that Jesus is God and lives in our hearts! This may well be what Buddhist and Hindu practitioners call the realm of all possibilities. There's something inside so immortal. This was my Mother's unseen sanctuary the place she understood better and communicated in and from effectively. This place was being unto itself and to her. It was in the flesh yet more than flesh. If that door was ever shut while alive she would be in the land of the living dead. Here structures would crumble from within. A living inner being gave her sense of purpose dignity independence -- this latter so essential to the visually impaired. She needed to have that kind of faith. Strength would come only from that which was living in her, a personal engagement which made her walk with confidence. I believe that after more than seven decades of chanting Psalms she became the prayer.

CHAPTER 38

The Priest

In our age of innocence and in the midst of select peoples and practices there was the priest who was feared and respected. Talk went that whenever a priest shook his black gown over anyone with whom he had a misunderstanding or conflict the person was doomed. The priest was said to have mysterious powers. Unlike today when the Dominican priest has emerged and continues to arise, those of the 60s were foreigners and White. His color never mattered to my Mother -- she did not mention it, neither was there occasion for conflict between she and a priest. In small communities like ours they behaved like celebrities. Not only were they seldom seen. Whenever they were seen, they wore the habit. Those known as soucouyants kept their distance. Those White men never appeared to smile and their services were generally boring. A Mother whose son became an acolyte was filled with pride and those who went on to become priests in the 80s implicitly handed their Mothers a ticket to heaven. Invincibility was assured. They would now be all protected from evil spirits. Their son knows every chant and the paths of the world under and above. Priests and ministers were so well-respected that any young man who chose such a calling was revered by his Mother. I was almost there. One Dada told my Mother I would be a good Methodist pastor/minister because I prayed so well in the Methodist church. My Father was not impressed. In fact, though he was baptized Methodist, in his later years his theological friends were Catholic priests. I believe he developed this lasting relationship with priests from his days at a Catholic high-school, his French training, and he being the only one in his Wesley community to speak French fluently. At high-school he worked as a scribe to Father Raymond Prosemans, one of the leading church historians of the time. Moreover, because of his Baccalaureate – he read Philosophy, Mathematics and Agronomy among others -- he felt comfortable conversing with the few Frenchmen who graced the island. But as for me being a priest or pastor? He didn't mince words over the matter.

The priest in a colony? He sometimes identified the forces while the obeahman prepared the concoction for those haunted by evil spirits. It was not the priest's responsibility to select the plants and herbs for preparation of the disturbed victim's bath. Today, few know of the closeness shared by the two. The obeahman smiles when he becomes acquainted with the source of the referral, lights the candle and mixes the Tarot pack. Politicians and prominent business people seek out and purchase his services. Internationally we do not speak about the obeahman but of an illuminati and, a group providing clairvoyant services to leaders in all walks of life. In many Caribbean societies the African gift of divination, much of which was lost across the Atlantic Middle Passage was blended into European religious ritual. Compound all this with the chemistry of the alchemist or the traditional or folk pharmacist. In this socio-cultural and religious ferment, Mothers were bound to attend carefully to their children's health and spiritual development.

CHAPTER 39

The Midwife and Mama's Teachings

The midwife was just as renowned. She traveled the towns and rural communities by donkey, horse, foot and boats along the coast. The midwife took upon herself partial ownership of the child. She was not the wife and in most cases the biological Mother was not a wife. In our days few Mothers were married. Part ownership would mean among other responsibilities keeping in mind and spirit the health of the Mother. It meant providing counsel to the would-be Mother who was expected to follow meticulously a prescribed act of nature. Other than her diet the Mother was to establish a communication with her unborn child. Others may describe it as an act of cooperation or communion. Mother also had to keep in mind that she did not want to be delivered by way of Caesar neither would the midwife then recommend an abortion. Caesarians were seldom if ever!

The midwife's work went on in silence somewhat like the dada. She was midwife nurse counselor nutritionist and trusted healer. She would sometimes communicate with the Dada on behalf of the nursing Mother -- to familiarize herself with all indigenous foods in support of breast-feeding. She had to be internist and dermatologist since the skin told her a lot about the health of mother and child. Indeed, the midwife's voice was a trusted stimulant to the ultimate process of expansion and contraction.

Does the Earth need a midwife. While the question suggests a critique of modern delivery methods and even technology, it embraces technique. It is not technology in itself that will deliver the Earth as much as how that technology is used and by whom. Of paramount importance is the presence of caring hands. Some critics of modernism contend that the Earth has been long experiencing pangs. I gather they are speaking of world systems "whose" Fathers are not around to take Mother on long walks along flat roads. World systems contemplate aborting rather than admitting the humane. Internal to systems is also an insensitivity to cries for alternative modes of intervention. World systems themselves may not want to deliver. The product may be dysfunctional and cost more to sustain than destroy or keep in controlled states of unfreedom. No matter the present range of discourse, Earth does not determine alone, neither will it be still in these times. Earth is being born again this time. But this is a discussion far-flung from the activities of the midwife of the 50s and 60s. She was a sheer composition of experienced gained, and applied intuition. She was not only about the process of delivery.

I recall one midwife coming to our primary school. Nurse Leoma Wilson taught each boy she could lay her hands on, how to draw back the foreskin and clean his penis. Boys needed that exercise in personal hygiene. Whenever she appeared we knew this was penis-change time.

It was like the dentist. He signaled pain, whether imagined or real for the entire day. The needles were long, the smell of anesthesia everywhere. The numbed jaw was excuse for not attending school in the afternoon. Then there was no preventive dentistry and a better sugar was not publicized as coming from fruits. There was an abundance of fruits yes, but also lots of home-made sweet things in tablet, coconut cheese, peppermint, and quite a variety of imported toffees. We eat all in this chaos of collective innocence, damaging our teeth.

Mumps measles and small pox came and left. Pox was healed in a crude yet effective manner. I had to go to the sea. A fire entered the open flesh.

Yes, there was injury and pain. Children were cut frequently by broken bottles and opened cans. Too often, many were ripped by rusting sheets of galvanize, pricked by nails attached to old boards and two-by-fours. It could also be a sardine corned beef or salami sausage can. stitching was painful. Children wore shoes on occasion. We had a pair for school and another for church. We did not always play with shoes on, though most of us had plastic shoes or rubber slippers.

Long before patches were placed in pants and sold at relatively high prices we did it ourselves. Every other boy could patch using a Singer machine common in most homes. Our clothes were usually oversized. Surprised. Mama said particularly about the boys that we were growing. Many of us didn't even know there was a prison under the name of Her Majesty's and, and crucially the oversize was an overlength -- not in the waist. It gathered at the ankles in an African Chief's style!

All boys cut their hair the way hair is cut today -- bald flat or short with a beebop at the front. In simple ways cycles of life are revealed to us. In grand style the future is the past. Within this context reflect on the Mothers who Fathered us, who mothered us embodying the father-figure.

On Black Entertainment Television's comedy series I often hear actors talk about what Mama used to feed them. Like us they had to eat whatever she provided. You had to eat it and not allow a bit to fall from your mouth as you filled it to finish the task. That was when she cooked what you didn't like. You recall when grandmother gathered all in one pot, how her food always tasted better. Seasons and celebrations, eating and drinking?

Christmas time we gathered stones from the bay-side to create pathways, circular designs in our yards. The earth had to be covered. Hail micro Stonehenge!

In the sixties we bought cork-guns water-guns starlites and bandits. We drank lots of sorrel and ginger-beer, eat cakes buns puddings fresh beef chicken ham smoked pork. As the years progressed my Mother as an employee of Geest Industries received an annual box of apples figs and dates from London or Barry.

In spite of meager wages Mothers gave their children a new shirt pants and shoes. It reduced the peer pressure. Even then children wanted to be in. Christmas was complete as was Easter. It was all about community interdependence. Theories of collaboration had not yet been formalized to guide organization of a Methodist cantata. Anorexia?

In those days it was good to be plump. I remember taking part in a play in which I acted as a King. As an excited teenager I invited my Mother. Despite her long day into evening she found time to attend that evening. When the play was over I asked her what she thought. She replied it was good but "I have never seen such a meg—thin—king!" Obesity now called globesity was rare. A fat woman or man was usually so handy that it did not matter. They worked hard. Fruits grew in abundance though I do not recall the habitual use of raw vegetables until the mid-seventies with the appearance of Rastafari/ Dread. In years to come they would make significant contributions to the development of nutritional and dietary patterns to the Caribbean Food and Nutrition Institute. Fruits were not a prescribed requirement.

In summer we lived by fruits alone. we did not have consumers -- that group of people other than those who sell and now eat everything from pizza to cell-phone waves and brand clothing. A history of the evolution of the concept "consumer" in the Caribbean, would make interesting reading, ending in the consumption of information over and above bread. In this telecoms environment, papaya is clandestinely losing its seeds in our island. Those who initiate the engineering are usually always foreign. They would select a night for tasting by the media and well-to-do in the hope that the acquired seedless sweetness would trickle down. In local markets, samples were scattered here and there. They were much easier for use in a hotel's fruit-punch. Though sweeter and better-looking they were certainly not as seed-filled and creamy as those growing in our neighborhoods. Fruit stories? We eat mangoes in whole.

While a student in Canada, a family invited me to Sunday dinner. As invitees entered the house the Mother allowed us to taste a rectangular-shaped slice of mango that she had chopped on a board from a whole mango. She said that's how she saw it done in Singapore. I wanted more. Most times, we pick it straight from the tree. Notice I wrote pick -- just how we would say it. We eat it direct. The mango is bitten from the bottom up. The top is the sweetest. It is an ecstasy an engagement a giving. The mango freely gave its creamy flesh. We progress along its entire curved body. The yellow-cream juice ran between the fingers, down the back of the palm -- most boys licking it! Anyone knowing mangos give their body freely, would have to suck it, lick it. Others when they peeled the skin off, eat it, holding the mango in hand as they chewed. Some swallowed others spat out the chewed skin depending on the type of mango. Want to hear those indigenous names sparkling in mango Julie, teetoo, long, bitterskin, leecka, mouleng, bellyful, kakapool, farine, madway? Exotic? In the case of a sweet Julie or grafted mango, the meat was eaten till we got to the seed and this too was sometimes scraped white by a few aggressive consumers using their teeth! Even Microsoft thinks this sentence animal and underlines it red. We picked them, washed them, bit them, chewed them sucked them, swallowed every thread of creamy yellow mango meat. Our defense systems were strengthened.

Since Dominica produced the most candy-laden banana in the banana world it would be unfair of me to say we consumed. We feasted particularly on the fallen bunch in which a snake was found curled. We grew up in a brave, wonderful world.

I do not wish for one moment to glamorize poverty. We were never hungry. Praise God for nature and our Mothers discipline. We were never naked. Our little house was always clean cool and a stop-over for those wanting a cup or glass of water. Oases are not always in the desert you know. We could not sleep in by virtue of the rising Sun -- we were forced out into the morning Light and Air, strengthening limb and lung. Those who stretched in morning's Light and Air -- our net-ballers footballers and cricketers -- our entire generation, just needed opportunity.

I did not know what my eldest sister was good at but my Mother's first son her second child became an excellent mechanic, emigrated to London where he worked as a supervisor with Ford Motors until his retirement and death in London.

My Mother told a story full of pride about her first son. On his way to London by one of those ships in those days, there was engine trouble. It is strange to me that that ship did not have its mechanic, but the expertise of any passenger was requested on the intercom, a passenger who could fix a particular engine problem. He presented himself, solved the problem and received a significant sum before landing in London. His recommendation to Ford was a fait accompli.

My Mother's third child was our town's first librarian and telephone operator. She died at sea -- strains of her disappearance are scattered throughout this return.

Mother's fourth child was an still is an excellent home economist in the days when it was a prominent science and art. At fifty she took up the television camera and shot outstanding flood footage which she had trouble getting paid for by national television. To this day she is a craft person, designer and finds a delicate interest in herbs and healing. She used lights so creatively at Christmas time that year after year for a while, she attracted the cameras of city television who opted to use her houses' thousand lights display as a model design. Just when she approached sixty, she picked up the acoustic guitar, took lessons, called me and played "God prepare me / to be a sanctuary."

The sister after me was a respected perioperative nurse and midwife at Holberton Hospital in Antigua, until she moved to Delano, California with her son, advancing the cause.

Our brother after her reached seventh standard at primary. He worked security with Ports and Customs, Dominica. He takes down, deconstructs the entire engine of any vehicle, places it together again and turns the key. Genius, I tell you.

Our last brother lives in Miami. He was once interested in engineering and electricity. He likes counseling younger members of the extended family, particularly my children. He worked with a wholesale food distribution company.

These children could have been many other things, professions. Probably they are already. I remember all of this with a quantity and quality of fondness. I mean, whenever our cow gave birth I had to move on to do the milking passing through those tall blades of dew-soaked grass. Streams ran clean then. I had developed such a love for nature that it did not matter how far away from home the cow was. It was, as a boy I understood the meaning of literal meaning. One morning I had a plentiful expression of milk from the cow. I was so excited. I was running home. The handle of the milk container came out and the milk was spread over the street at my feet. I was standing in running milk. I heard a lady say "don't cry. Mama will not beat you." I arrived home with the empty container. My Mother having heard the story, looked almost proudly at me and said "this happened to me when I was a child." I simply could not pick up the white-cream liquid. It defied putting together. Some things in life are just impossible. Mother's calm, exemplary response over such a crucial income earner, baffled me. We sold bottles of milk to a small clientele mostly within the extended family. Moreover, since we each had something to barter, share, we all had something to eat. I think Mama understood this much better than I ever did, yet she did not fuss over the fallen milk. Thing is, of the one hundred ninety days on which I went milking, the milk fell once. This observation was made by her in an instant. She saw my face, the empty container. Mama was constantly teaching me something.

I feel sometimes that this narrative ship has drifted too far from port too far from its captain's preferred course. But it doesn't matter anymore. Mama is not going to hate me for it, neither will my brothers and sisters accuse me of leaving out so much.

CHAPTER 40

Get Tough Mama Suggested

I travel on a stream, and there are times when drifting is adventure. I write this and thoughts rush almost competitively to surface, shouting speak me, write me. The drift wins, not in the context of the dwivayez, nuances and subtle, even dark energies, but this time in memory of years when ships were not heard of for days, men returning dazed, with carnivorous tales having sucked fish blood cooled in salt water for survival. I had never been this far in a drift, eating raw fish and stuff. Though my Chinese friends tried to get me to eat a variety of Japanese raw salmon -- sushi they called it -- I could not make the grade. Don't like raw fish.

Hey, let me tell you a real drift story when Mama sent me out to sell agricultural products. Thing is the engine on our sloop named Patience, gave up on occasions, sometimes at the back of St. Maarten. There was no breeze either. The deck was scorching. Where I sat while we waited for Wind was where I stayed. I could not shift. There is a period of inertia in a drift when everything is still especially when the sea is calm. In those days there was engine trouble. When there was no wind the main-sail and jib went flat. They just stood in the white expectation that the Sun would see them on fire. When wind returned it was strong and we had to reset our course. Choppy resistances propelled the sloop.

While waiting for Wind I heard stories of sailing adventures, reviews of island politics, stories about women, relationships, sex and good times. The stuff was heavy and I, I thought myself too young to participate. I listened. The social political and cultural emerged in the drift. One older sailor maintained a memory bank of recollections that he delivered in a rated language. The language of the sea is brutal. How fishermen became saints remains a mystery still! It was in this milieu that Mama chose to send me, selling. My imagination took flight. The law of the Sea is not the law of the Land. First principle! It is a habitation fraught with dangers and beauty. It is an awesome place. Nothing is clearer in my memory than a full moon rising on open water, no land, just water for miles and miles and miles. Mama. There was silence too schools of silences porpoises barracudas and sharks. After a drift, porpoises, those known scientifically as belonging to the phocoenidae family, sometimes sailed with us numbering twenty or more. I don't know whether they witnessed our stationary position, lurked beneath our hull, or as friendly creatures stayed close to immobile objects on the ocean just in case life emerged from them. They communicated, I thought. Or maybe they always moved in community. But they surfaced. They surfaced as soon as motion began, swimming with us as if happy that we were on the move again. I love that mammal. I use to look forward to seeing them, their dark beauty energy joyful playfulness and seeming bursts of laughter. The speed with which they swam together would startle any boy or girl. They leapt out of the water with atomic energy -- when they finally departed I would feel a certain sadness as if I had lost a friend. There was that will to jump and be spirited. Their brisk movements made me laugh from my belly. I was once ordered removed from the front-deck because I was more interested in the beauty of the mammal rather than its cooled flesh. That day when one was harpooned I was ordered to leave the deck in language deadlier than my Mother's anatomy. I, an adolescent, made the mistake of asking why should anyone of the porpoises be killed. It was hit, harpooned, and began moving feeling pain, the foreign object in its body. It heaved. The cord attached to the harpoon was unraveling at great speed. The sailors decided on a block and tackle because the schoolboy refused to be taken. I knew it would die but I loved the fight. We were heading for Sint Maarten and were about five hours away. You were going to take me, I thought I heard the porpoise say but I am not going to make it easy for you. The calm dark-blue depth around us began to redden at surface. Honest, I was frightened, terrified by the onslaught. I understood there was money to be made selling its flesh, but the process by which the porpoise was being taken, saddened me. Mama, a sailor does not have to be so sensitive. In my heart I screamed, resist school-boy, resist. Break away, burst the frigging line. But the harpoon was deep and, block and tackle strong. There were times when they would pull it in and it would swim with all its power, I imagine, unwinding the rope, gaining some slack. They would release the slack and roll the winch again. The porpoise would come in again, then break loose again. It was a struggle in which one of the combatants was wounded in her or his habitat with a foreign object deep in its body. Its wholeness was broken, its surface, its inner organs on Fire. They were going to take it, but not without a fight. Porpoises do not die without a fight, no, not these energy-filled mammals, those glistening dark-blue beauties of the sea whose eyes seem to laugh when I look at them. I'll remember you, the eyes appear to say, never full of pain, but with power of constant alertness to the fight to the finish. The schoolboy was drawn in along the watermark and would not let go of its life or will to swim. Ropes were tied and tightening around its lateral parts along the center and as long as it remained alive, three men could not move it from the watermark. The block and tackle creaked. Cutlasses came out. Six or more schoolboys swam with their dying partner. The others stayed a little in the distance submerged halfway. As the sloop heaved in rising chop, blood shot out of its pure powerful gills. Choop, choop, choop, choop. Blood shot, shooting. Two of them proceeded to stab it still with the harpoon in it. By then the others in the group gathered around it but the sailors could not take another. They had spent hours taking one. As we drew closer to land, after four hours, it began to expire. Slowly, sorrowfully the others swam away as the land rose out of the sea. From my vantage point I wept. I had witnessed a sorrowful goodbye. They stayed with their brother or sister until he or she had died. And still in the circle of spirits others waited until they had arrived. Who knows: the Mother might have been swimming along the water-mark.

At St. Maarten, the schoolboy fetched a great price. Its deep-red, blobby flesh sold real fast; people there feasted on it. They didn't know. They didn't see. I thanked my Mother for letting me go to sea. When I got home and related my story, she only looked at me with those daring, adventurous eyes and smiled, knowing that she had already made arrangements for my return north.

CHAPTER 41

Delighted Mama Sent Me

In one week, I was off again to St. Kitt's with plantains tannias oranges dasheen. These sold well on the Basseterre bayfront. News seemed to travel fast that there was fresh produce from Dominica on the bayfront. People came to buy.

I remember the bag tied to my waist containing those Eastern Caribbean dollars. A fifty-cent piece was heavy silver, and a five-cent a golden yellow. Notes were larger too and carried only the face of the Queen of England. I write this, and see myself stepping into a Basseterre bank to make some change, as we say, before the rush began on the bay-front. Beautiful women in the bank -- my Father must have affected my perception in this matter. He lived in St. Kitt's once, and told me I might have a sister there, but I did not know yet to look for traces of a henry or her Mother's name. I just remembered the young teller serving at the bank was gentle-speaking, shapoti color as my Father would say. She must've been fascinated by my dark, oily smell, my black tam, black electrician's boots, blue jeans, rubber around the wrist, thick knotty hair uncombed, blue sweat-shirt, lean body, hands long, fingers signing with calligraphic skill. "Who is this dirty intelligent young man," she asked. I thought it a compliment, salt and erotica in my eyes. Told her our ship had just arrived with some produce, selling on the bayfront. She smiled. "I guess I'll have to come this way later in the day to drop off a hand of plantain for you," I asked. She was overjoyed and I, I loved every teasing edge of her smile and teeth. Friendliness? All that I brought ashore at St. Kitt's sold. It was brisk. The people knew that each week the boats from Dominica came to sell them excellent agricultural produce. They could buy one or two weeks supply. In those days, I sold a pound of plantain for sixty cents. Two plantains weighed a pound, and I had ten bunches, huge bunches. I was free, not stingy with the scales; you know I gave a bonus, spirited the buyer. Didn't know their names, though I heard them calling out to each other. I came to know their smile; one they gave when satisfied. It was good, standing on that shore, darkened by the Sun, dreams in my eyes, dreams on water. I saw each tannia, each hand of plantain go, and I, I simply had to call out to my ship-mates that I was ready and they'd row ashore to pick me up and my bag of money. Remember, I had to drop the hand of plantain. Albert, you know I wouldn't miss that! The dollars were not yet in order, you know, fives with fives, tens with tens etcetera. I just placed them in the bag at my waist, having a section for coins only. You know my banker arranged them. To this day, I love St. Kitt's, Sugar City, present headquarters of the Eastern Caribbean Central Bank, managing the braille-inscribed, thread-updated modern representation of my large Eastern Caribbean dollar, its fifty cent and golden five cent-piece, its copper pennies and haypennies.

From Sugar City's delight, we would sail across to St. Maarten where I would sell jelly-nuts. Coconuts went real fast. People drank the water and eat the white meat right there. They loved Dominican coconuts; it maintained its freshness.

Those northern islands thrill me; things sell, sold fast there. Still, there's something about St. Maarten that to this day captures my imagination. Could be its white sand beaches; I had never really seen, really seen those. You know humans: we call them white, but they're not really. Don't know why. Maybe I had never seen a street on which only jewelry was sold. That thrilled a teenager. Gold, gold, everywhere.

It is a place I hold preciously in my psyche, though topographically, it is so different from Dominica. There's a wetness about its aridity and stone. There was always, always a light, an aura of possibility. Then, there was no university. It was the port of rest and offloading. From here we would sail back to Dominica, maybe touch down at Anguilla for half a day, but from St. Maarten, after two or three days in port, after I had consumed large chunks of my thousand-page novel, it was time for home. The Shoguns were popular then. After a day's sale and offloading, I just pulled up at the bow, couched myself in the lowered jib as sunset passed, reading, lifting my eyes from page to water, amber to page. I had to wait to get home to clean oil, smell of diesel and sweat off my body. Fingers turning pages as patience rocked softly had their nails clipped to prevent injury. The sea? It was at sea that I practiced not sleeping.

In the days of the comfortable Swedish steel-hauls, named Bo and Mireya, I slept. I almost slept through a storm in Martinique's channel, until I was awakened by what appeared to be water at Mireya's port-hole, water full of lightning. On Patience our sloop, sleeping space was right over the engine if anyone wanted to sleep at all. This was used sometimes by two or three female hucksters who took the trip home after their sale. They might have flown up but decided to save some money and sail down. They suffered in those rough waters as the boat rocked and rolled from side to side. I would hear them scream sometimes when it was really bad. I recall us stopping in St. Barth's, a French territory, a hideout for actors and actresses. Its coved beaches are so dramatically exotic and its rum so cheap that by the time we were ready to leave we were up for excitement -- there is exciting sailing when the sea offers some playful resistance, wind being sufficient. All goods were delivered, produce sold, fresh fish broth on fire whiskey flowing. That day from St. Barth's I had a drink too. In the east we sited another ship heading to Portsmouth Dominica. It was PM Bill. A race was in the offing. We received a tremendous lashing from the sea choosing to sail south against a squall coming from the east. PM Bill went East Southeast angled into the squall. It was good Wind. Wicked swells. The women were screaming. The main-sail held West, coveting squall's wild serve of a constant wind. In this savage milieu of water, spray, stinging salt, wind would sometimes come from the West, swinging the boom East. The man at the tiller had to be ever alert as the boom swung. I sat low on deck, yes, on deck. Wet, unavoidably wet. There was nowhere else on this sloop. Waves rolled passed me like a mountain to a child. I no longer vomited, having adapted to the rock, roll and thunder. Our helmsman, our winning rated story-teller, took us through.

From this early age, I learned to respect simple people. Here was a focused drifter usually permanently drunk, unschooled yet capable of working a ship through such storms with shouts of joy when our sloop tilted, dived, rose, held on a side with perfect speed, rise and fall on an ocean that was a thousand times its height and width. His compass was in his head, in sounds from the Wind and mere outlines of land. God. You are so mysterious. Where you place your skill is no man's to decide. Jagan. A master steersman. He, with salted eyes, took us through. From the northern mist, sea spray and fog, Dominica's north coast rose ruggedly defiant. While our sister ship was hugging the land we were to the west. This was home. We sauntered into port, our sloop white, I, walking from side to side. Seafarers, hucksters and musicians would become my better friends. I didn't know it then, but Mama was putting me to the test, making me brave, enriching my thoughts and imagination. I was learning business too, working hard to pay for my education. I needed to learn to support myself. "Is this yours?" Mama always asked.

CHAPTER 42

Mama's Dying Draws Me Further Inside

My thoughts flow in a stream of consciousness. I am on a journey that engulfs releases embraces terrifies loses makes me despair fills me with passion excites me, teaches me almost how to keep silent or manufacture it. I can feel when there is a disconnect and encourage it knowing that in the world of consciousness there is surfacing there is emergence, there is a coherent coming in. Clearly, this narrative gave me the rocks from left to right making me drunk -- It throws me off balance. I understand swagger in the sailor's step. Along the way and, I must say it is a way, I think about significance of this text in New York or anywhere other than in Dominica and it does not matter. It is a wavelet in the ocean of consciousness. It is an island story with some meaning for anyone who has lost a life or lives. I've learned in Life there is the unannounced arrival. The glimmer of the call in the eyes of those who are about to leave us is remembered only after the fact. There is a greater force at work. What is even more wonderful is the return of our departed in dreams and visions telling us stories, showing us places handing us objects, revealing to us our deeper world behind the office space the bus and train. There is a place in us, in blood and bone and breath. We must purify the breath purify the thought purify the heart purify the mind. Indeed, our God is a consuming fire! This purification needs be urgent especially when the departure of the loved-one was tragic. Those who leave us in old age, leave at a time and season that is relevant to our unfolding life -- those who celebrate the departed as culture reveal wonder in and of the risen Christ. I became aware of that which is contained in me: truly, there were days when my spirit was so close to an awareness of the perishable nature of flesh and blood that I was overwhelmed, thinking, even feeling that I was about to die. It is the call to be fearless. I have to, I must die to an old self. To be honest I do not know what the emerging one will be. What I do know, is that in mourning there is healing.

CHAPTER 43

Religion Tells Me No

While our Mother was at the funeral home (in a condition that we all hold and know to be true), I requested from the Catholic priest in our hometown of Portsmouth permission to say a few words at the final ceremony, on behalf of the family. I was told that this was allowed only in the case of figures of state. His secretary had handed me a one-page proclamation from the Bishop of Roseau outlining reasons for the non-inclusion of statements from non-Catholics. In silent laughter I uttered to myself: I thought I was a state figure who had contributed significantly beyond the call of religion and politics, to the development of my country to be trusted in the delivery of a few words on behalf of a woman who had weighed every truck that ever entered the yard of Geest Industries in Portsmouth carrying hundreds of thousands of tons of bananas feeding a community of thousands of households headed largely by single women. I realized that Canon Law did not know our history. To add injury to insult, the resident priest told me all the things I had to say, I should have said to her while she was alive. Hmmm.

It is amazing how a priest can sometimes sound like a police officer to a civilian a doctor to a patient a teacher to a student an insurance agent to a consumer. Two months later, Elizabeth "Ma Pampo" Israel, allegedly the world's eldest human died and was given a state funeral. She was buried in the same cemetery as our Mother. I forgive these people. Indeed this is a celebration of oneness in the Spirit. Yes, Mama, your broadcaster Son, I who spoke excellently to thousands each day for more than a decade in the name of my nation's development was denied the privilege of speaking at your funeral. Religion. On November 21st. 2004, at about 7:45 am, the same structure in which I was not permitted to speak on behalf of my Mother, was destroyed by an earthquake!

CHAPTER 44

Therapy in Wisdom

Lebanese poet Kahlil Gibran once said in order to find the secret of death we must look into the heart of life. Heart of Life? Death is one tree growing in the garden of Life. One of the shapes or forms that Life takes on is flesh, blood. It is intricate and wonderfully whole. Simply place your finger on the pulse under your ankle just above your heel. It is the gentlest of spots. It pulsates the delicate nature of Life and makes me laugh. Yet within that body are such diverse streams, billions and trillions of cells, neurons, fibers still undiscovered. The entire standing form flows blood in its oxygenated surrounding. A fish is at home in its habitat. A human being should be in and under this vast awesome space moving its weather its seasons -- hard-pressed but not crushed. There is night and day. It can be cold and hot snowy and windy. Breezes are cool on the face blowing twisting hair. Water flows in abundance in places and mountains reach into the skies lifting our eyes. We bleed when cut and cry when hurt. I have seen a sword's point pressed against the belly of a monk and the sword bends. The human body has inherited secrets that we are yet to fathom. It is such an amazing creation. It can lift off and fly. A body standing on the floor of Wall Street's Stock

Exchange might have had a balanced breakfast but is no different from the one standing on the deck of a ship awaiting passage of a squall before settling down to eat from the fish caught before the weather turned ominous. The ankle strained at the World Cup is structured the same as one twisted in a banana field or by a dancer in South Africa Chile or Bolivia. Citing Aldous Huxley, my Father used to say, if we grant theism the logical outcome is monotheism.

There is a sameness about us that we have abdicated to a differences discourse. Who gave shape to the skull of an Iraqi child or fashioned feet of an Afghan woman. Is the wrist of a Palestinian made of stone and the finger of an Israeli straightened in cartilage. Is the brain of a Zimbabwean cast in steel and that of a Briton in alabaster. Does an American taste with his eyes and a Spaniard with his knuckles. What causes a Saudi Arabian to think that he can destroy Yemen's city of Sana'a or, an Israeli, the bones of a Palestinian child? Of the fourteen million teenagers worldwide who give birth to unwanted children annually, which one carries her womb in her chest, and her vagina in her mouth. When has a fish ever given birth to a stone. A sameness you will agree is in flesh and blood bone. The body changes dies rots. Whatever is different in all of us does not grant the option of a state other than death. It is a passage. I hear the screaming that culture makes the difference. Not to death. Then language makes the difference. O, the most beautiful and nuanced ones are disappearing or have been subsumed. This rush of breath along vocal chords and tongues -- for some critics a major determinant of reality -- does not say hold to its breath when its captain lifts anchor for a heavenly port. Truly I am yet to see a Caribbean man or woman with their hypothalamus in the palm of their hands. You behead any man woman or child and they're dead. You cut off their feet and they can live. Every body placed in the Earth rots. Each melts in Fire. As far as I know a thought has never been exhumed neither has a feeling been the object of an archaeological discovery.

Papa used to tell a story about the making of Man. He meant woman and man, the anthropological kind -- what the Vatican calls humanum. God, he said, had an apprentice watching carefully as slime, mud was slapped into place and transformed into flesh through the potter's fingers. When the structure was completed it did not move. It seemed to have no life. The apprentice wondered: how was this thing going to be set in motion. God knew the eagerness. The fascination was clear to the Creator of that said apprentice to whom the wait seemed eternal. God touched the apprentice and he went into profound sleep.

Secret, mystery of Life? God then blew the breath into the form; the structure and it began to function to move to walk to run. When the apprentice bounced back into the wake state he discovered mobility. What's gotten into it, the apprentice wondered aloud not in English of course. The body was alive, activated, its parts with or without names. How did this motion take place? Was something placed in its mouth? Did it eat something? Nostrils, the Universe whispered. And, even when the apprentice heard, breath's birth remained unknown, hidden in the Creator. For sure, if anything was eaten by this form running now, that breath-food had to be supportive of and easily converted into flesh blood bone. If we accept the biblical rendition of Creation, we will agree that the air was clean. Think of those lungs pure fire in those bones. That heart was not under attack. There was no hole in the world no ozone layer had been depleted. In telling me the story we did not come this far and the Eagles had not written in song about the state of the world's natural and social environment. I asked the morale of the story. The old man left it for me to work out. He revealed later that the apprentice would become Satan knowing structure of flesh and blood. See the power of Christ Jesus taking back God's mysterious creation by giving up his body and blood? Christians call it precious. They have a point. Through a sacrifice God took back the original artifact known in toto by the apprentice to be flesh and blood. This you would agree is still largely unspoilt eco-physicality, if you wish; habitat to which we have few measuring chants, though they're right before our very nostrils. Surgically open bodies. We discover something other than what we went in search of. It is no longer in the tomb, no longer subject to physical corridors in flesh and blood, visible yet invisible. It's in the rainbow. It appears and disappears at will, moves to another rhythm, Original Mother Song. Hollywood is yet to respond fearing religious intolerance. Hollywood should've stepped forward long, loving as it does the subject of death. Is this a different kind of transition, one that poses refreshing technique challenges for the old image-making paradigm?

It was through death that the real matter was completed. Not only were flesh and blood and all that is contained secured. There is dominion over death. And just when you thought Hollywood had enough to digest, Jesus rises from the dead! This is a massive project for virtual reality!

Does it matter whether the body type is pitta vata kapha. Yes a body that is fat muscular or lean responds differently to emotions or digestive processes. Different body types thrive better using different diets. They may not require similar levels of vigor in exercise, meditation, relaxation. Does the resurrection take into account body type. Not at all. Does knowing our bodies and possibly their types enhance our living. It certainly does. Does that determine when we die. Not at all. It is true however that our bodies are temples to be cared for. I can say people in our Mother's generation cared their bodies and more. They would say, thy grace is sufficient for me. It is letting go, trusting, believing, receiving the spirit of immortality, allowing that spirit to move their mortal, guide it, give it strength, instruct its humble questions and answers, more so in times of hardship, when sound decisions are being taken.

Breath was introduced into that body by the Divine Psychologist as his apprentice slept. Breath hit blood bone. Thought, emotion, action electricity. Motion. Wow. The Old Man's story. Action, thought and emotion are interconnected.

Art Of Living teacher and meditator, Dominican Anthony Toulon notes that at the base of thought is emotion and patterns of emotion. Compassion and love are profound intelligent emotions. They are generally not depicted by ice or cold, but warmth and Fire. This is said to be in the human heart connected to head, head to feet, warm. Remember cold feet? Bi-polar? Dysfunction, split, separation? A killer whose crime is macabre is often described as cold-blooded. True love is always warm. The body that gives up its breath becomes cold.

The form standing in Eden in the old man's story became warm when it was set in motion. The body that dies returns to the heat of Earth. Ultimately, it returns to Fire at the core. Then there is the question of blood and or breath. They are both mobile active in flesh even among atheists. The dead body carries blood hours and days after it has been pronounced dead, days after its breath has left it. Breath itself is a rather busy traveler. Breath has a vast, FAR-flung bandwidth a tremendous information holding capacity. Deepband. It may well be Life's principal blueprint. It never dies! When its vessel dies it finds another. Blood needs breath in a human body, yet breath does not need blood to fly. Breath can unannounced leave flesh and blood. Yet there is something wonderful about blood. It is a culture medium says Bruce Lipton of epigenetic fame. It reports to Earth. More lightly, it provides evidence of its existence. Have a conversation with it!

CHAPTER 45

Five Senses and Structure

We who gather to pay last respects to anyone feel the course of emotions as they rise and fall throughout the place of worship. The body lies still yet the breath into which every human being is initiated moves hovers with its own information. Indeed, it evidences yesterday and today -- it bears substance of the peace we hope for. We know, however that there are more violent exits.

We thank God that we ourselves could place our Mother's body back into the Earth. We did not have to try to identify her among thousands as victims in a violent earthquake or pandemic. We did not have to live with the memory of her having flown out on an airplane that would later crash over mid-Atlantic waters. She was not caught in the cross-fire of a coup d'état and her body buried in a mass grave, neither was she the victim of hunger so terrible that her family was forced to move and she in her age died along the way. You may say does it matter. It certainly. We believe in seeing our dead before they rise! Does that mean that those whom we never find do not rise? Certainly not. Call it vanity if you wish. We love to touch them before saying goodbye.

The breath blown in us has left her body. It is in us still. She herself prays that we be steadfast in love. As Mother she wants us to continue living remembering gifts of her own life, examples of resilience and faith that works and moves. She wants us to put all this to work toward the improvement of our material well-being. It would hurt her to know that we were living as what she so graphically described as fish out of water.

The old man's story grows in significance when one considers birth of a child. She enters another less enclosed world and breath enters her nostrils or should we say the baby was greeted by breath. To a fetus the world from which she came might have been large and diverse. Contact in this place was close like a fish in water. This may be quite unlike humans who are not always aware of the closeness of our universe, its Air wrapping us constantly touching us as we sojourn on Earth in the sky with no mythological Atlas, just free breathing, free flexing. Touch. There is the possibility too that the breath was in the child to be activated only into this Earth-scape. Who set the breath in motion. The Spirit certainly was not visible. The midwife did not have the interests of the Old Man's apprentice. We may say also that since the Creator and his apprentice are invisible then only the Creator witnesses the delivery and blows or directs breath. This is beginning to sound hilarious. Who said that the apprentice is invisible too. Who grants such power. The apprentice may as well be alive and dead in many forms other than human. Truth is the modern child is under attack from its conception. Think of the apprentice wanting to make one standing, running, laughing -- my God, think of laughing, just laughing. How did Creator cut, shape fingers, those bones eyes and heart with such precision? Look at the feet how they do not bend, fall, seven holes in the head, the inner ear, the body's liquids, the stomach to the central nervous system. How the body's named and unnamed parts connect, interconnect! He wants to create one and set in motion too. Set in e motion?

Smell must have been paramount. Today it's visual. In the days of Jesus it must have been the ears. Taste was always, until it became for fine clothes. Touch is still out in tones though it was used wisely.

Five senses? Who watches visits the lab daily for hours as the child is being formed in the womb? Who shakes the womb mixes its chemistry over and over, takes its measurements and speed of formation? Who invests patterns of emotions? Who gives love "as an emotion," to cite the Jamaican Reggae band Third World? Who maintained the temperature of the room? The final word belongs to the keeper, owner of the lab. Seems to me however, that the apprentice has come to know an additional something over millennia having experimented with emotions outside the lab where he earned his first degree. Consistent with the Old Man's story, is he now master of the five senses? Of the fourteen million children worldwide who give birth annually, who watches as they are being criminalized? Who watches zealously as a young pregnant Mother injects heroin into her veins or who or what exacerbates the condition of a Mother who is HIV positive and, who watched as a syphilitic master slipped into the vagina of a virgin slave laborer? Slave labor and the old man's story of God and the apprentice? We've arrived.

They saw a machine. It did not have intelligence. It had structure and structure enough to lure their masters omen-kind to naked raw villages in heaven. They had structure to respond to lash and chain to hit with rhythm. They had structure enough to be, to stand in international fora on justice and hear the names of others called for rewards and they, forgotten or so it seemed. They know something too about the apprentice. The Old Man's story says a lot about expertise of the apprentice and the simultaneous power in restoring, of God who searches out the heart and mind of the spirit. The story shows clearly what the apprentice used to have control over. The apprentice finally lost control over death! He held control over the artifact that died thinking this to be the end of the matter, but the property was not his own though he had laid claim to it. He knew that at its core was a place, a room, a breath sanctuary, a Holy of Holies that would not die, that he did not know how to open, create or kill. Just when the flesh and blood project appeared to be under his control in its descent, breath moved the form he knew, lifting it up from Earth's gravity, causing it to fly; it became lighter than cotton.

I gleaned from the Old Man's story that maybe we should not underestimate the apprentice's knowledge. Food can be prepared which changes behavior. Those fifty years of age, trapped at the adolescent level, develop plausible arguments justifying their desire. War becomes the action of choice for solving differences. Women and men see hate as delicious as a platform from which to launch their bombs and reasonings. The composition of thoughts that we call mind has been invaded. Thoughts of self-destruction bolstered by promises of an entourage of angels lead men to self-destruct. Guns are turned on each other without the slightest thought of consequences here, emanations beyond. The murderer is locked in a single, monotonous, tunneled chant to kill. The businessman curses the rain wetting the window cleaned just half an hour before the downpour began. A child is senselessly raped and buried and a woman's head split with an axe by her jealous lover. Fear controls nations and leaders turn to evil to sustain their iron hand. Whole corporations fall on account of one corrupt leader and those whom he has intimidated into silence and restless privacy. It's time to breathe out.

CHAPTER 46

Mourning through Autumn

Tell you, New York's October autumn Wind is terse as I step out in the daylight stretching across a blue sky teased by white clouds from the painter's brush celebrating Fall. Leaves huddled around gates and street corners waiting for a wind lifting branches with uncontrollable laughter. Dandelions lie low in silent enchantment while birches rocked overhead howling fury in places where the Sun had tried to scorch with Summer's eighty degrees now forgotten until another shift in seasons another death in snow, distant now and not subject to the speed that depicts New York life with its sirens fire trucks mowers and a ceaseless montage of car into truck into train into planes fading into sports utility vehicles rumbling out of their parking like ocean waves far too far now for instant view yet still memorized in sound waves, and pliant muscle. I had reflected so many times on death or falling leaves with approaching autumn that I actually picked up leaves, to speak to or with them or at the very least allow their cells touching my fingers now eager, to learn to tell me in languages of my Mother's silent passing, joys and pains in and of the season even as I mourned. Still, when I did not hear them speak, the very act of picking them up, looking at them and thinking that we communicate, was sufficient to spirit energy on that afternoon of October 15, 2003, when a fast-moving New York ferry left Manhattan for Staten Island carrying hundreds.

The Andrew J. Barberi crashed into a jetty on the Island. eleven were reported killed and seventy-one injured. Two were decapitated and an undisclosed number amputated. The pilot was said to have bolted from the scene and later tried to take his life. There was talk of fatigue and a throttle failure. It was noted that that seaman at the wheel was a man who had received numerous commendations. What could have taken hold of this pilot's flesh, skill and blood? At what point did the throttle and its material composition change? Can material objects be affected by forces other than their own mechanism? What could have caused one of the passengers to leave the lower deck and go to the upper five minutes before the crash thus preventing him or her from losing leg or head? Could someone in Manhattan have called his cell causing him to walk to the other side of the ship because he could not hear on account of strong winds? What if the captain had pulled out of Manhattan three minutes earlier? Talking leaves? Death is always in the Air.

When an eighty-one year old woman dies it brings an outpouring a strength. It is not marked by the kind of weeping that accompanies the death of a decapitated Mother or a twenty-one year old woman who jumps on to a trains track to retrieve her fallen cell. Earth can speak of three thousand at the World Trade Center, Hundreds of Thousands in Iraq whether by others or by their own hands, Six million Jews, One Hundred and Ten million Africans in a North Atlantic Slave Trade and, Ciboneys, Algonquins, Arawaks, Kalinago/Caribs, Mayans, Aztecs, Christians, Buddhists, Hindus, Muslims, Ugandans, Congolese, Rwandans, Armenians, Cambodians, Japanese, Vietnamese, Lebanese, Afghans, Iraqis, Kurds, Libyans, Syrians, Yemenis and billions before them. Indeed, these are the last days! Not only is death always in the air. It is at work in the body. The apprentice has made a mark. They say, it was left to Christ Jesus to show us that death was not the end of the matter. The apprentice's detailed knowledge of the body would not suffice. Beyond within the structure there is more. Outside its quadrillion cells a field breathes Fire. In truth within the mortal the immortal was blown. Indeed not only has the apprentice graduated. The Creator has brought this power over death into the mortal form that it may live as if death did not matter, caused no fear doubt depression anxiety. The problem is there, but it is no longer a problem. We can now live new lives assured that we will be restored in Christ. That was my Mother's way of life.

Historically her people not only fed sugar cotton and tobacco fields. They cultured resurrection's liberation in the midst and thick of exploitation. There was chattel, muscle power. There was a promise, an energy flame in chattel that at times would reach overflowing anger directed and justified. Those who brought the word never dreamed that the immortal breath was deposited, eco-moving too under those black skins. In that environment transformation was inevitable even when they stood still or moved. Not only did "I think" become an active principle. "Therefore I am" emotionalized, rushed blood made fearless by breath and victory over death. This will forever startle the master who now has a master himself since "I am" has broken from its ramparts the black ship from its moorings. In the midst of this created, natural chaos there are attempts to reduce our cause to a common delusion, dismissing the fact that what was one hundred fifty million gold Francs of Haitian money then is twenty-one billion United States dollars in the first decade of the Twenty-First Century. Silence!

I calculate it to be seventy-four days since my Mother died. I find myself needing silence and a change of life. I began to examine my actions closely. I wanted to change what I did not like about me. There was anger which I needed to direct. It was OK to be angry. What I do with it is what matters. There were times I realized that my fists were clenched and set them loose. My Mother used to lock her strong fingers in a vice. The less active and mobile she became the firmer the claw. I would try to open the hand and they would eagle-claw almost as if they were formed that way. The battle was on. The apprentice shuts down the hatch. She decides to burn, sink the damn ship. They take her to the deck to get some fresh Air. She jumps into the ocean. She surfaces when they draw the rope in for sending and submerges when it is sent. They would discover that it is difficult to fight someone who is strong, one not afraid of dying. Death is not the problem. There's something inside oceans know, ocean receives as one. But to live? I knew I had to choose life. This is what my Mother would've liked me to do. Yet besides her wish, or should I say, in addition to her daily example of living life, I wanted to follow her disintegration. Point of entrance, was it not? I realized this to be impossible. The idea when expanded and deepened carried a lesson a review of life as I live it. Her death began to mean start of a new life.

Along the way the tracing felt cold. The dead were not the business of the living. Leave them alone. The best you could've done for them was to love them while they were alive. This was not the context in which the priest and I negotiated. It dawned on me that I was going deeper than I was indoctrinated. In a wisp of arrogance I felt that she was My Mother and I could do what I wanted with her fragmenting remains. Together we claim the body. What would be the purpose of such a venture except writing itself? What would I have learned inside a narrative imagining chunks of a forebrain inside a skull melting in Earth's Fire? Poetry. God's detail, the kind never to be exhausted.

Why is it that all that remains is skeletal. How did this reduction happen this synthesis in bone so hard to last thousands of years. We're finding them in Ethiopia and, in Australia where Black people with cotton hair lived long before the British tried to make the continent a habitation for prisoners. ABC reports that those finds in Ethiopia were 160,000 years old. Ethiopia? Let's touch Sudan, Kenya, Tanzania and South Africa! Silence!

CHAPTER 47

Mourning's Comfortable Thought-Moments

Reflections on her passing and burial led me to other places -- exploration of their finds did not seem to me to be unjustified. Her life was more than just her disorder or her dying. Her ideas dreams and visions alive in my head, my memory, affected more than just an umbilical sensitivity. Though requiring me to move them, they went beyond what I believed as Rational Man. The raising from the dead is not a rational matter neither is life after death by way of Christ Jesus. In my time I've seen and heard great men impact the course of human life and history using ideas primarily. St. Paul, from creation's wisdom body, says Christ Jesus was a blood sacrifice. That was not of a goat sheep cow elephant or whale. It was the sacrifice of a human being designed in that period of human development to conclude an argument over who has power over death. This was more than a paradigmatic shift. Paul was exceptionally salvatory, redeeming, restorative. But you as well as I know there were and are some other men, with different intentions set. How a few could have come almost fifteen hundred years later to destroy and shed the blood of another race of people in another world, even as they preached Christ Jesus, is clear evidence of the ripple effect of a perpetrator's curse. They came preaching a Word, obscuring truth, Truth as old as human appearances between Earth's oceans. By the time their Word reached maturity in lies and theft, it was no longer about blood. We could no longer settle. It would be Fire. And, just when those perpetrators thought history and God were dead it was more Fire! This softened the steel. It opened the mind. Fire tuned the pan. Did you not know? It is in blood tuning! Breath finds a broken bone to tune to wholeness. The baby may be said to have been spirited by its encounter with the force. We do not know whether its entry or activation hurts causing a sudden yet brief cry. Response to a blessing may as well be a cry. All who hear the cry rejoice and know it to be Life. The child is welcomed into community, a collective breath, God's desire. Indeed breath is in the bleat of a lamb. It is nuclear.

A tree is cut to shape a casket -- the tree itself breathing its own weight in the forest its own mythology sucking howling voices in Wind. The Sensay (a Dominican carnival costume) is fiery. In folklore of the carnivalesque it is said to communicate with spirits in the forest, those pithy whispers in the Wind. How trees love the commonality of human flesh and blood. They melt with it; these tall biodegradable protectors of soil, producer of leaves, healing to many who believe, truly believe when walking beneath their communicative oxygen.

A tree surrounds your body Mama as it is deconstructed. It is varnished and smoothed yet its substance is the same sap hardened like blood in bone. The seven holes in your head will soon be reduced to a zero factor itself a circle too universal to have any other than one as its immediate digital partner. Breath in the fire would've hardened your cheekbones and immaculate skull. Utilizing all of these, plus that illusive sense of touch has proven sufficient for one civilization. We take it for granted but if you are to reflect on what a person sees and hears in a lifetime Mother Earth is overwhelming. There are others, places in this universe but none like this stage called Earth. Earth produces and reproduces itself yet it is not its own, neither does it belong to us. We belong to it. With mathematical precision it touches neighbors, those described as cold uninhabitable, haunted by hurricanes blowing for hundreds of years, constantly erupting red, milky, those unformed still in the womb of another time -- the handiworks. Have you seen Mother Earth's natural forms, its rolling hills under sunrise its tallest mountains its fjords its deserts bodies of water crashing white, the only white I've ever seen. Have you ever seen or heard a herd of bison run, witnessed diamonds pour out from a spade a landmass over calm seas as shadows fall. Have you ever seen a woman weep as her children are lowered into the ground. Have you ever noticed beauty under her tears sorrow, a purifying Fire burning still in the midst of all this madness!

No camera, said Mikhail Gorbachev, can capture the emotions passing between two people when they look into each other's eyes as their cars approach the stop-line, cool of an autumn morning. Truth. Truly, New York's autumn morning is cool, refreshing. In the distance I hear a ceaseless rush like shallow ocean waves and I realize it is the sound of vehicles in a constant uniform flow. I whisper: God protect them as they rush. Silence. If only we had the opportunity to hear that sound again but silence is gone from here. It is the resonance of presence. It is a form of sedition.

CHAPTER 48

Mourning's Silence Lessons

When a nation's people remain silent while their leaders corrupt lie and deceive, their silence says loads about the insipid nature of ignorance, the catastrophic power of instilled fear. When people have a right to talk and that talk results in nothing changing, though they voice their concern anger frustration, this is silence. It may be described as silencing. The Neville Brothers of New Orleans captured for me what I was thinking in that American Autumn Air, when they stated "its freedom of speech / as long as you don't say too much."

Speech begins with my first cry. I do not have to be told it is free except if someone intends to restrict it. That freedom is based on the premise that speech is wise true wholesome bringing good winds of change. In fact there are those among us who believe that to speak is to do, so powerful is the act of speaking among them and the wisdom traditions to which they belong. Wise speech is not forgotten. My Mother used to say to me if I am to find faults in you I will not stop. So do not look to other people's faults. She would place her hands on her lips whispering to me, "you talk too loud." She should live here. She even told me I talked "too much" forgetting that I talked for a living. Truth is she wanted me to own the speech-gift property, care for it, respect its divine origin. Whatever I had as material thing from the days of my youth, she wanted to make sure it was mine. She guided me to find not only my own material, but my own inner property, to know and feed freely on the fruits of my mind. I remember even as a grown man I owned a lap-top. When she saw it for the first time she asked "is this yours?" Straight to the point, Mother to Son, even then.

Silence. A city has a language. Where it sprawls was once a forest. Though its trees and hills are gone, Wind still travels the same course. This time it does not electrify sap in their rings but genius in their architecture. Bridges roads waterways tunnels. Silence. This dancing body is architecture. Breath in the buried bone is in the hold of the buried ship. Yogis par excellence. Silence. The city is a dancer. The city is a Sensay reveler connected to the spirits of the forest in Wind. The dancer spins shakes quakes in creative memory and steeled muscle. Silence. The city is taking her body away to cover it with branches and tales of pollination. Silence. If I were to speak I may say something that may resonate. Silence. Where is the sensual coo. Is it now left to the stage screen, black-sand beach lovers, or potters palms? Listen. Resistance. Women who faked period pains in cotton and cane-fields, men on a go-slow, the look in their large black eyes as lash fell on bodies responding with a story fomented in drum codes over cod salted beef given today withdrawn tomorrow with Pavlovian dexterity, dreamed in color, rage and sun. Awake! Resist! They dreamed awake with eyes that saw the fork in hands that see targets in evil eyes looking back at Them afraid too but for different reasons. Those rebels knew the length of struggle. Their masters saw the short-cut. Silence. Those men of learning in the civilized world did not think that the body in the field dragging a cart identified a learning curve, held strength in numbers and patience. Those long lines of humbled antecedents deposited working faith in the very hearts of their progeny. They were the sacrificial, structured in heat, mercantilism and industry -- an undeniable faith in that hidden quota reserved for the next generation's loins. They had to be skillful to maintain tolerance and channel anger even as they fashioned victory in the image of God. Those vessels had to hide that technology of simultaneity while delivering labor and increasing production. They were not supposed to sweep sands of consciousness across the Archipelago's chain. Their captor oppressor knew how to control Earth's resources but very little about promise in Truth's energy. Indeed, before justice could fall on them in any cataclysmic, in any catastrophic way, they had built their cities and waterways, established their institutions and healing centers, manufactured governments kings and queens shipping and science constitutions and laws, controlling vast territories. At the center of classic exploitation my people surfaced. Through spirit and Fire for creativity, they strategized, rebelled. Yes, we would later watch them come again, conquer divide rip off destroy cover up and leave. People in my Mother's time applied the Word and Gospel to the situation. Silence. They had consciousness scrolls to deliver.

In the days of their prosperity no ailment in the body prevented them from delivering, meeting, greeting -- no sudden storm no blinded eye no strained back no sore no quantity of poverty no lack no darkness no false report no foreign preacher no dog fence or barrier no prosecution sign no decree no list no adjustment of their social and economic structure rooted in the hand, lending a hand, no gun no flooding river prevented them from sharing their love. When one member had all members were satisfied. Even over distance they felt, sensed more readily any attempt at harming a family member. Amazed? They looked out for each other, developing a communication having nothing to do with the oppressor, never mentioning her or his name, confident in their space and its own references, positioning themselves knowing that what mattered was not so much how much they made but how well they were. They watched the enemy's intentions fade, die while they praised the Lord, while they rejoiced. Even though they knew miracles of return, they worked rejoicing time, worked rejoicing to the stars when the enemy faded, fell. Their lives advanced beyond economic gain.

There were weeks when the market economy was in our favor. There were weeks when it was not, even as our fruit got better. In silent amazement we watched as productive fields shrinked from ten to five acres and the rules and regulations governing marketing grew increasingly enigmatic. We gathered and spoke but there was no action. Our governments had condescended into extremist modes of not knowing only to hit a bedrock harder than their uninformed confusion. Silence. Transnational methods are divisive. The process is clearly revealed by departure time. They leave destruction as they leave. In fact in a few colonies of the Dutch kind, spirits haunt mansions still as they rot. The free West Indian space was fair ground for the occult and those Europeans were no simpletons in the expression of their I Am. Over time so many healing herbs plants and fruits pronounced poisonous after specific experiences they might have had, turned out to be right for many contemporary ailments. Fruit and seed-bearing trees were gradually replaced by beautification symbols. The haunted artifact would be visited less and less as it retreated under forest trees and an abundance of stories fomenting ignorance, superstition, striking fear and causing slave-designed architectural traces to remain undiscovered, undisclosed. Silence!

CHAPTER 49

Mama's Favorite Psalm

This has taken us to a sanctuary. This is one of Earth's churches ruled by ritual and peoples Love. Mama's God-daughter is a singer at her funeral. Mama's brother is her grand-father. She sings mama's favourite Psalm 27 and needless to say, I am captivated. She's deep like a baritone. Silence holds the congregation listening. An African-American southern presence is combined with a Caribbean gospel swagger filling a Roman Catholic church in the Caribbean with this chant older than Mussolini. The congregation sits still hanging on to each note every repetition of whom shall I fear. Atomic energy. None of them can stop the times. In this first stage of Life if you hear repetitions sufficiently systematically they become believable. This voice chanting the 27th Psalm, will be heard this time and this time only in this style and accent. It says "when the wicked, even my enemies and foes came upon me to eat up my flesh." They were not cannibals. No. They were not pariahs. They were not even vultures or vampires. They were enemies, all of them!.

In the single room of this woman, now dead, were the echoes of a chanted psalm. In this psalm, her enemies stumbled. Christ crucified and risen might've been the stumbling block. They did not only stumble. They fell. The voice ascended as her euphonies rumbled sweetly. Now, right now, I hear a voice speak another Mama's favourite: "you shall not be afraid of the terror by night, the arrow that flyeth by day, nor the destruction that wasteth at noonday." That such an ancient text should be so perfectly placed in our time and context is noteworthy echoing the prophetic insights of the 91st psalm and the unchanging yet shifting nature of human conflict. The range of current military hard and software is displayed in part in media, in this ancient extract, from suicide bombers to snipers chemical and biological agents surface to air missiles to drones, hey Mama, to underwater cameras and clones. Plagues cannot be forgotten.

The choir sings "Another Mountain." Almost immediately I hear that this life is the first life. There is another passage. Thank God it will not be another Middle neither will we be alone in the all-consuming Fire. Quite unlike those who came to teach the love of God in Christ Jesus this Fire is not the one sold in the Hell market. It is a purifying spring in which Jah lives. Hmmm.

I am in a process here that excites me. I constantly lose and find flow of the text. Every time I identify what I intend to write it moves away. Every time I look away from it, it draws closer to me. Mama. I read this engagement with the text and its flirtation as Love. In its sweep and wrestle its tug and battle its fright and bravery I was humbled. The text says to me those you love do not always love you. It is those you do not look to who tend to love you. In essence, this brought to mind the biblical eye situated in Romans 10:20 and Isaiah's 65th chapter. "I revealed myself to those who did not ask for me; I was found by those who did not seek me." The text gathers deceit lies honesty and intelligent life simultaneously. In its swoop it catches a double-faced image speaking a double language that it converts into one. It is as ancient as it is modern. It is like seasons, consistent. It is like Wind which has me wondering this Autumn morning whether it will blow as vociferously again Today. Has Mother nature ever been negligent? From where I stood, I tasted in the Air pleasures of childhood -- so freely did I wonder. I couldn't tell if leaves had been sufficiently shaken and wait nimbly on time to fall offering me another look into their palmistry. But I know Fall's riotous bursting, its night winds moving a million leaves along middle streets needing only shadows for horror to figure. At night, wind is drama when bearing Autumn leaves. Mystery season celebrating falling; mystery season of which I am a student.

CHAPTER 50

Waves of Mourning Return

From a yard in Laurelton, New York, I reflect further under these grey skies. Rains are beginning to be heavy in Dominica at this time. Its elfin vegetation will soon be thoroughly covered in mist and cloud, its rain forest thickened by thunder's lightning. The spot where, the spot where our Mother was laid would be soaked. Seeds and flowers planted or placed on the site as decoration would've taken root and blossomed. The tree in which she was buried would've sounded its entry into melting. Flesh and blood would've begun giving up their identities to rotting. Her voice will be heard in her children's voices. In eyes like mine you'll see her eyes evolving. She is now a passing thought in the minds of those who knew her, a figure constantly present over those she birthed. Her love is even stronger toward her grandchildren whom she loved touching. Yes, the blind touch with hermeneutic precision if these two are ever achieved together. Forensic science is gonna have to pay for that talent. In her living last days, when she wanted to know how much our children had developed she would ask them to draw closer to her bedside. She felt the back of their thighs then their backsides and took their hands as if weighing, weighing their strengths. When they met her approval along the way, indeed, on the scales, a smile lit up her face and it usually did. She uttered good she spoke the positive. As for memory, that was all she had until the last two years when she began privately shifting her attention to that other world and its demands for a concise life summary. Touched by the ever-moving she began to edit, dump the garbage holding on to what she thought mattered as if it were a water bottle or goblet, a few Bible verses a song. These would condescend into silent streams and trickles of quiet running. She listened now. There was the cry I heard during prayer time in the mornings when I was with her: out of the depths have I cried. She had tasted life's many precious things grown on Earth and yet had a deep desire for something more: the love of God in Christ Jesus. Death could only change her form not her substance. The spirit which had come to dwell among her people, witnessed successful implementation of its message of charity, strengthening encouraging and comforting of others. The rest is left to God's saving grace. What great sense of taste!

CHAPTER 51

The Gift Death Reveals

It has been said somewhere that wisdom is tasted. I think the same of breath and the Sun and thank their Creator. From behind my eyes, the Sun bursts in all glory. I consider the Heavens, the work of Jah's fingers, the Moon and Stars. Without the Sun, we're dead, all things are dead. And that Sun shines from between my eyes breaking forth over horizons, running silvery sentences that nurture this emptiness as I mourn. I am replenished. In silence, I see each day another world, another place teaching. I learn when I let go, become part of, live with, sip from, dwell in, coexist, thrive, rejoice. All is in motion and like all, I am!

Evidently, the great Sun pours forth light each day with or without me. The Moon and Stars pour forth speech with or without me. Without me what goes up still comes down. Oceans crest and trough whether I'm here or not. Rivers course, nudge banks, create deltas, turn oceans brown, flood, root boulders from their beds. Whether I am here or not, these forces roll on.

It is the energy-breath in every part of me inside that speaks my time. When it and its fire leave, I'm dead. This is the end of the matter. This is the equalizer. Father, into your hands, I commend my spirit, my breath and more. This breath holds an energy secret for us. It was Pope Frances who reminded all in one of his 2015 encyclicals that contemporary man has not been trained to use power well. Training. Let's begin now to use that breath to guide and nurture our own to Wisdom Territories. Power well. We use it but to what end, for what purpose? This great gift that death reveals is tantamount to the resurrection power. What happened? How is it that we did not cut that path? We give energy to our machines yet this body stands in perfect proportion, fragile, easy to bend, flexible, waiting for us to say to that breath in us, let's do it, let's move into you, open up your sanctuaries, your mansions, your gift to blood, bone, cell and protein. Yes, we are created thus -- called to our highest selves heaving already in us. And it's all of us. I thank God that I have brothers and sisters whose very embryonic forms drank from one place, took shape in that place, on that bed of bone, flesh, blood. When our Mother breathed we breathed. We, all eight of us, drew life from her inner being, drank from what she drank, breathed when she breathed. Indeed, we reached for the same breast having smelled its closeness! Even when our Fathers were different, a common thread runs through us. It is the Mother-thread, the Mother current, the Mother chemistry. She looked on each of us with brimming delight, so close was each tender mouth as it gripped her nipples. Even when our Fathers were different, we laughed like each other because we had the same Mother.

It is good to give thanks as long as you are alive. The 206 bones that stand you now, started somewhere, at a specific time, in a special place. There is no civilized and uncivilized sex. We cried, griped, teethed, dribbled, had our noses cleaned. This woman from whom we ushered, whose waterbag broke had many bags in her, many bags capable of growing in her. To each of us she witnessed the fashioning of one to our need, size, shape, intensity. Hey, who knows, one might've been fashioned after our calling, our good and perfect gift. Let us, all of us in this world, remember that even if we were born of different Fathers, our Mothers are the constant. The Earth brings forth all things that feed her and she feeds us. Earth itself is Mother, just as Africa is said to be the cradle of humanity. Well, before humanity got into the cradle, he and she had to be born; possibly drawn from the waterbags in the Nile or delta of some fecundity. Mother figure. Today, we are being bathed, approached by feminine. We are enclosed. We are already surrounded. The vast ocean does not crush the sprat. This vast high-energy universe feeds us, will not crush us, makes herself known to us in the midst of zillions of others. Oh, well, let's be serious here: that which was fiction is now truth. The Nile is no longer distant, neither is its waterbag. Wow! Mama!

CHAPTER 52

Vingt Sur Vingt/2020

I sit in a university hoping to draw meaning from images bursting behind my eyes. When our mother used to say she saw writings on the wall it seemed strange, even deranged to us. In 2020, I am writing as part of a narrative inquiry discourse.

> "{I}t is a justice call to engage the gift of an inner sensibility that continues to deepen in the adult learner's dimensions of knowing through intuition, dreams and familiarity with the mind's eye. In truth, it is a complex pattern of colors such as violet, indigo, blue, green, yellow, orange and red appearing as concentric circles of color, or as a combination of rich color pulses flashing against a white open space similar to an ocean into which distinct black shapes appear, change and disappear. The shapes, always in motion, blend one into another or change to another completely different from the first or second. What impresses

me about this flow of images, shapes and symbols is that they were not meant to be seen as much as they generated a feeling of participation -- you are watching me and I am watching you in a community of motion. Justice. Truly, to live with glaucoma is to experience days of fog, mist and darkness on different days, and sometimes, both forms of opacity in one day. The fog is not as close as days of darkness can be -- there are days when the darkness is so thick, it feels like its choking. Unlike the darkness, the fog or mist, or white is generally in the distance. There is a space between me and the overwhelming white distance ahead of me, with one defining line appearing as a horizon. Along that horizon runs a silver lining. More recently, however, phases of darkness have begun to have the silver or white lining that can be golden when in vibrant motion along the full stretch of this perceived horizon. Words can fill the line of that horizon, but when I try to read them, they disappear. They are to be impressed, not to be owned as vocabulary. In truth, brain and mind culture a wonderful relation. Thus, the vague and nebulous depict a beginning that may be still, but soon gives way to objects such as spheres, whole indecipherable passages, symbols, animal such as herds and birds, living creatures of the ocean and eventually celestial formations in motion. This is the case whether the eyes are closed or opened, though the images are more marked when eyes are closed. Could this context as a whole be described as a seeing ecology or an ecology of the eye? Are these objects, animals, places, faces and bodies a historic resource showing other ways of seeing and knowing which when understood can calm

> the seer and knower? Do I not have a right to think these given that the system of care no longer cures?"

I took it upon myself to transform this visual impairment into a study. Lesley University in Cambridge, Massachusetts accepted me to pursue a PhD in Educational Studies with a specialization in Human Development and Learning. I wanted to find out how adult learners who are visually impaired or blind learn.

As expected I went by way of imagination and of course, my professors suggested the concept of active imagination. In fact, my original concept was that of "innervision." Yes, I am completing this program learning through hearing and the use of a screen reader; my books all electronic and held in my laptop. Lord, I kept a rich library once, a library of actual paper books!

When I need to go to Cambridge from Atlanta, I get in a wheelchair at Hartsfield-Jackson airport. I am wheeled to the plane, board, led by an attendant on whose shoulder I place my left index and sit. I lock on seatbelts and relax. The attendant comes to me to ask if I need anything; she even brings me a book in braille. I try not to drink anything while in flight. I do not want to have to go to the washroom. Depending on where I sit, if at the window, it is inconvenient, if on the aisle seat it is easier, but I try not to have to go to the washroom.

When I arrive at Boston, someone from Delta or Jet Blue comes with a wheelchair to pick me up and wheel me to luggage pickup and exit. My host is waiting and we head to her house.

It is another matter climbing the steps, getting to know the ways in that house, the descending inner stairs, doors, seats, the washroom. I must select my clothes without an eye that sees color. They must be organized in particular patterns when I am packing to make sure their colors match at the very least. I must set down my laptop, shoes, combs, toothbrushes in the same place each time; place my shirts on hangers and feel their textures to know their differences.

I am transported to the university by my host who hands me over to a sight aid who spends the day with me in class. When a video is on for demonstration, the professor comes close to me and describes the visual. I do not see what is around. I hear it, touch it, smell it. Hey, I even taste its air. Voices become clearer to me each passing day and thank God, I remember.

It is difficult but I have converted this blindness experience into a joyful learning experience. Am I interested in a cure after more than two decades of placing drops in my eyes? Oh yes. A cure is coming! In the meantime I capture the psychology of blindness. I note the emotions. Indeed, I delve into the world of vast images, a world that is not generally revealed through the physical eyes. It is one I am so happy I came to know. I thank Mama.

I no longer hurt over loss of sight. I've discovered a galactic dimension, what my Jamaican friend Dr. Leanora Ruff calls a conceptual environment that acknowledges works of wonderful ophthalmologists, optometrists and vision scientists, yet presses on to another field of interest beyond the biological, the physiological. It may be considered a big assumption, dismissive, or running away, but this running away is surely not one away from the self. The imagery is to evident, too repetitive, announcing itself and its presence without my calling, intention or decision. I have become part of a world of images that I must learn to interpret and understand and present to the world my findings in that conceptual ecology. What seems like science fiction today will become science and humanity soon. It is not long before our vehicles become silent even while in motion!

CHAPTER 53

Thank Mama

I thank Mama for this one major move in my life: she told me at 19 to go meet my father. Now, that was powerful, beyond comprehension. Here was a woman who had had four children when she met this man. He was nine years her junior. She developed a relationship with this French-educated Dominican who had only just returned from the northern French department of Guadeloupe. The contradiction was not more dynamic: he was from English-Creole speaking Wesley with a French education. The people of Wesley do not speak French just like the people of Antigua who constitute the larger family of the people of Marigot and Wesley. But here he came, coordinating time at the building site of the Portsmouth government school just about 100 yards from our mother's small house.

The narrative runs that he left her and me when I was about four or five and went back to his village of Wesley where he would live until his death at 55 in 1986. Thus it was that after Mother had pulled me through six years of high-school, after I began teaching at a Catholic primary school in our town, my Mother recommended I should go look for my Father.

Now I had seen him many times before between seven and twelve. During every conceivable holiday, but particularly during summer, my Mother would send me to Calibishie, a village a few miles from Wesley, to be with my aunt. My aunt had two daughters and her husband was a forestry officer in the northeast and chief scout commissioner. The house of the forestry officer for that area was located above the Calibishie police station. It was a structure owned by the colonial government. Those things aside, I would be sent to be with my aunt every summer for sure.

Every other Sunday, my aunt and her family would drive to Wesley to attend service at the Wesley Methodist church where she played the organ. Hear those influences. It was after service while driving through Wesley or on our way from Marigot that we would meet Fred Alpheus Colberg Henry walking along the roadside. My aunt's husband would stop his jeep next to the walking gentleman and say, "Stein, look your father." Fred Henry would look in my direction and ask, "you're alright boy," and I in gentle innocence would answer a soft yes. I would be seated on the back seat between my aunt's two daughters who were big teenagers by then. These were the times when I caught a glimpse of the man who would become the most significant influence in my life on Earth. When I left high-school my Mother asked that I go look for him.

Over time, as we grew accustomed to each other, as I fitted into his minimalist existence, he would ask me two questions which to this minute guide my thinking attitude. The questions were, "what is faith," and "what is mind." A Father asked his son those two questions in 1975 and transformed his life forever. It did not matter that he did not support me materially. When once in a letter I inquired about this support thing, he replied in French: pour autant que je sache, la vie est remplie d' erreurs, mais pour moi tu n'es pas une erreur"/ "as far as I know, life is full of errors, but to me, you are not an error." I have read and repeated this over and over in my head and each time its love goes deeper into my being. Very soon, I will capture our relationship in a separate text, as the old people say, God willing.

My Mother could have been bitter after his departure when I was five, but she did not harbor those feelings when she saw possibly a hunger in my eyes. Not only were they her eyes; they were constituted too in a sense of passion and wonder for knowing. That would be satisfied by my Father.

CHAPTER 54

Matters That Still Linger

It was strange to me when I read once, "{I}t was good for me to be afflicted, so that I might learn your decrees" (Psalm 119: 71). I came to know much because I humbled myself and opened to the possibilities of seeing. And they were greater, much greater than the physical act. Now, do not get me wrong. It is beautiful to see the world, but when sight has been lost it is even more beautiful to move into deeper seeing. Find that novel space opening to you. It seems strange initially, but as you foray, ask, seek and knock, you discover a dynamic ecology and environment where all that is witnessed lives in harmony. It is really Earth's reality in a galactic vastness, farflung, dangerously beautiful, deep beyond our thinking and imagination and loving. Earth has, as a living being, been through journeys in this vastness and a grand reunion has begun. It is from the breaths and mouths of babes and sucklings that we hear the message. We can either move or change or we will be moved or changed. Even the Earth knows the season and time. These movements and changes are manifesting now behind eyes to our delight!

Even as I write, Glaucoma Research Foundation is writing about a "catalyst for a cure." Gene therapy is the buzz-word among professional members of Canada's Fighting Blindness Canada. Blindness should not be!

I pray that my brothers and sisters, my children and grandchildren spot this sneak thief early and knock it out. This has proven every time to be most effective.

Find that food for the brain. This too is the way that those researchers at Vanderbilt University are pursuing. There's hope even as we find out that glaucoma is a disorder of the central nervous system. The journey into the third eye, the pineal gland, and the ajna chakra, has moved beyond those physical manifestations. I came to know these and a world steeped and shrouded, if not clouded in the language of medicine. Still, those medical practitioners in ophthalmology are discovering pathways to restoring sight; some too proud to stop saying there is no cure.

What has happened since my mother's passing? She continues to come to me in dreams. Nothing's wrong with that at least not to me. She always instructs, warns and indicates time to move in time of indecision. Even at this age mother still instructs with authority. I let her. I do not resist, sensing a wisdom body, a person or spirit larger than clusters of mere matriarchal responses. Our people of African descent serve as our cloud of witnesses: they teach. She's still in my laughter, movements of the arm, in my walking and listening. She listened. I still practice her call to forgiveness, to distill the matter and deal with only what's relevant and benefits all parties. Time is of the essence.

My two sisters Pearl and Joycelyn and my two brothers Albert and Ernest are alive. Joycelyn and I have grandchildren now and Pearl, Ernest and Albert have children. It is an amazing motion. Life moves on and at some time, I too shall move on and another shall come and move on. May their preciousness be protected and advanced!

Indeed, one of the most beautiful things my Mother did for me was to connect me to my Father. This is not only a complex sentence; it is a revealing one to write.

I still believe I could have done much more for them. I have been informed by the most informed that I did sufficient for my parents, but for a long while, I remained haunted by feelings of not having done enough to make them happy. It is one of the strangest ways through which I remained bonded to their memory. I would discover later that that tension between them and I was necessary to complete their influencing me. They just did not want to leave and I, I could not tear away so simply. But it was what I had to do, not by will, not by might, but by the spirit of the Most High God. Mother no longer disrupts. She just appears with a message to my dreams. So much for my love for the collective unconscious, my brothers and sisters and our children and grandchildren; indeed, the communities of Zicack and Portsmouth, Dominica, which gave me primal life and force! Its soil beneath my bare feet, its breezes, light and water, its space, our play, laughter and cloud of witnesses returning again and again now! What assurance! America comes with me to this salubrious space. How abundant!

Jan 28, 2021
208 Walden Walk Dr.
Stone Mountain, Georgia
USA 30088

www.ingramcontent.com/pod-product-compliance
Lightning Source LLC
LaVergne TN
LVHW021957161224
799262LV00012B/143
9781954941342